Bad Words

Bad Words

*A Legal Writer's Guide
to What Not to Say*

David L. Horan

CAROLINA ACADEMIC PRESS
Durham, North Carolina

Library of Congress Cataloging-in-Publication data
Names: Horan, David L., author.
Title: Bad words : a legal writer's guide to what not to say / David L.
    Horan.
Description: Durham, North Carolina : Carolina Academic Press, 2023. |
    Includes bibliographical references and index.
Identifiers: LCCN 2023038706 | ISBN 9781531027704 (paperback) |
    ISBN 9781531027711 (ebook)
Subjects: LCSH: Legal composition. | Law--United States--Language. |
    Law--Methodology.
Classification: LCC KF250 .H67 2023 | DDC 808.06/634--dc23/
    eng/20230929
LC record available at https://lccn.loc.gov/2023038706

Carolina Academic Press
700 Kent Street
Durham, North Carolina 27701
(919) 489-7486
www.cap-press.com

Printed in the United States of America

Contents

Contents

About the Author

United States Magistrate Judge David L. Horan took the bench in the Dallas Division of the United States District Court for the Northern District of Texas in November 2012. Prior to his swearing-in, Judge Horan was a partner in the Dallas office of Jones Day, where he led the firm's Issues and Appeals Practice Group in its Texas offices. Before joining Jones Day in 2004, Judge Horan was an associate with Hughes & Luce, LLP, in Dallas.

Judge Horan received a bachelor of arts degree in government and philosophy, *summa cum laude*, from the University of Notre Dame in 1996 and, after transferring following his first year at the University of Chicago Law School, a juris doctor degree from Yale Law School in 2000. After graduating from law school, he served as law clerk to United States District Judge Janet C. Hall in Bridgeport, Connecticut, from 2000 to 2001, and as law clerk to United States Circuit Judge Patrick E. Higginbotham in Dallas, Texas, from 2001 to 2002.

Introduction

This is not a book on how to write the first draft of a legal brief or motion. This is a book for editing the second or third draft, when you should cut out material in your first pass that, on reflection, you have decided should not be put in front of a judge.

This is a handbook to check anything about which, you wonder, is it a good idea to say that—or to say that in that way?

This book offers a guide to words, phrases, rhetorical devices, and at least one punctuation mark that you should not use or should at least think twice, or even three times (not "thrice"), before using—or overusing—in formal legal writing.

Most of the words—almost all adjectives and adverbs—aren't bad in every context. Many are not bad in every legal writing context. But they're all bad in at least some ways that legal writers use them.

Avoid adjectives and adverbs for better legal writing

My principal advice is to use adjectives and adverbs—as well as legalese and other five-cent words and phrases—as rarely as possible.

That's easier said than done.

Here's an example that looks a lot like what I have read and, at some point, written. Consider the first sentence:

Plaintiff has utterly failed to establish even a single genuine fact issue and, in his wholly deficient submissions, has clearly offered absolutely no evidence to support his entirely meritless claims.

And the second:

Plaintiff has not established a genuine fact issue and has offered no evidence to support his claims.

From a court's perspective, nothing is lost between the first and second sentence other than some length and 13 words that the judge did not need to read, as this marked-up version of the first sentence illustrates:

Plaintiff has ~~utterly failed to~~ <u>not</u> establish<u>ed</u> ~~even~~ a ~~single~~ genuine fact issue and~~, in his wholly deficient submissions,~~ has ~~clearly~~ offered ~~absolutely~~ no evidence to support his ~~entirely meritless~~ claims.

The second sentence with those edits is more, not less, forceful, because it conveys confidence in the point that the writer is making.

Almost any sentence will carry the same meaning if most adjectives and adverbs are deleted. And these words often are red flags that the writer is overstating her position. Understatement is almost always better.

I practiced law with Glen Nager, who had a personal rule banning all footnotes in his briefs unless there was a strong reason to use one. (A great rule.) Legal writers should consider imposing on themselves the same standard for using adjectives, adverbs, and legalese.

How this book will help you achieve better legal writing

What follows is a guide full of adjectives, adverbs, and other words and phrases that you should use less often, rarely, or not at all.

This is a book of advice on improving legal writing. And the advice as to each word, phrase, or rhetorical device (which are listed in alphabetical order in a dictionary's style) provides some food for thought on if, when, and how often you may want to use any of these words or phrases.

Legal writing is a specialized subset of formal writing. Many observations in this book apply to other types or genres of writing because good legal writing shouldn't be alien even to a reader untrained in or unfamiliar with the law.

Why better legal writing matters

I love legal writing, admire any good writing, and have no doubt used many of these words, phrases, and rhetorical devices myself while in practice as well as in orders and opinions since taking the bench.

And I know that the practice of law is challenging and difficult, that it is harder to write a short brief than a long brief, and that it takes more time to write something that is short and respectful but persuasive.

But it is important to strive for that standard and to avoid the temptation of writing something that you would never consider saying to an opponent's face or in a courtroom.

It is important—that is, good legal writing matters—because you are trying to persuade your audience to accept your client's position. And successful advocacy requires effective communication and avoiding things that may cause a judge to lose confidence in you or become distracted or confused or annoyed.

Effective communication in legal writing entails submitting shorter documents that include shorter sections with shorter paragraphs and shorter sentences and shorter words. Shorter, that is, than much of what you have read in legal writing in your career so far.

Legal writers should write shorter because judges are busy and need to get through briefing efficiently. And that means filing shorter motions and briefs and not taxing judges' and their staffs' time or attention wading through SAT words or, worse, checking a dictionary.

You have probably heard this advice before. It is hard to carry out.

But the easiest way to make progress on this goal may be to use shorter, plainer words with few, if any, adjectives and adverbs.

That is the positive case for following this book's general advice.

Here is the negative case: Writing with lots of adjectives and adverbs amounts to telling, not showing. And showing (not telling) is far more persuasive.

If you believe a defendant is a thieving crook, provide the court with a dispassionate account of the facts of how and what he stole and swindled, rather than a string of inflammatory descriptors.

If you believe an attorney is dishonest and breaks his word, lay out in your brief or motion a detailed chronology of the instances in which the attorney failed to abide by his agreements and promises, and let the court determine that the attorney has acted in ways that the court finds to be untrustworthy and unethical. Better to have the court write up that finding in an order or opinion based on a factual record than for you to use colorful language and angry words to try to make that case.

Writing with lots of adjectives and adverbs facilitates unciv-il (and ineffective) advocacy that distracts from telling the judge your position on the matters that the court must decide. Judges don't welcome lawyers' "prov[ing] the adage that the substance of a motion is inversely proportional to the amount of hyperbole and rhetoric it contains." *Knepper v. Equifax Info. Servs., LLC*, Case No. 2:17-cv-02368-KJD-CWH, 2017 WL 4369473, at *2 n.1 (D. Nev. Oct. 2, 2017).

If you don't believe me about all of this, you can look to the advice of the author of some of the clearest and most concise opinions on the federal bench, United States Circuit Judge Frank H. Easterbrook.

In a 2012 speech honoring and recounting what he learned from former Deputy Solicitor General (later United States Circuit Judge) Daniel M. Friedman, Judge Easterbrook explained that

> Dan Friedman insisted on plain talk using simple words. That's a vital rule. Any private practitioner can and should do the same—though pulling it off requires careful editing with the goal of simplifying and shortening briefs. That was Dan Friedman's goal in reviewing.
>
> His style was bone dry. He went through a brief and deleted almost every adjective and adverb. "Very" and "massive" vanished. No instance of "clearly" or "plainly" or "simply" escaped his red pencil. Good thing too. "Clearly" signifies that some question has just been begged. If you must say that something is clear, it usually isn't.
>
> Adjectives and adverbs designed to intensify a point actually weaken it. Instead of shouting at judges through intensifiers or exaggeration, use the space for a better line of thought.

Frank H. Easterbrook, "Friedman Lecture in Appellate Advocacy," *Federal Circuit Bar Journal* 23, no. 1 (October 2013): 9. There's a lot more. You should read all of the guidance that Judge Easterbrook offers in that published speech.

And the judge follows his own counsel. A review of 80 published opinions that Judge Easterbrook authored and that were issued between March 1, 2020, and May 16, 2022, shows that, in those opinions, Judge Easterbrook did not use "plainly" or "massive" or "obviously" or, with one exception (other than when using the terms of art "clearly erroneous" or "clearly established"), "clearly."

I know that most of us cannot write like Judge Easterbrook. I cannot write like Judge Easterbrook.

But all legal writing would benefit from all legal writers trying nevertheless. And hopefully this book can help with that effort.

How to use this book to improve your legal writing

While my advice so far should sound familiar, this book goes one step further, laying out one-by-one—starting with a "Top 50 to Avoid" list—words, phrases, and rhetorical devices that writers should use less or not at all in legal writing and explaining why a word, phrase, or rhetorical device should be avoided as much as possible or altogether.

Concerns about wordiness, obscurity, overstatement, ambiguity, weasel words, and incivility—and the idea that language ought to be pleasing to the ear—underlie much of the counsel throughout.

Unlike a dictionary, I intend for legal writers to read this book straight through.

But, like a dictionary, the book also serves as a desk reference in which legal writers can, after or instead of reading the book from cover to cover, look up words as they're drafting and editing. I've included at the end of the book the cleverly titled Alphabetical Table: Where to Find the Entry for Each Word, Phrase, Rhetorical Device, and Punctuation Mark in this Book to assist legal writers in checking if a word is included and, if so, where to find it within the book's three sections.

Writing will always be more an art than a science. No one can offer a mathematical formula for landing on the best word choice or selecting an appropriate tone.

But I hope that the advice offered here may go some way to helping legal writers avoid using fourteen words when four will do—and do better.

If this book helps even a few lawyers perform regularly in their writing as their best selves, it has been worth the effort to advance the cause of making all legal writing more effective and at least a bit more civil.

David L. Horan
Dallas, Texas

Bad Words

Top 50 to Avoid

My principal advice for improving legal writing is to use adjectives and adverbs as rarely as possible. The second section of the book includes a dictionary-style collection of words, phrases, and rhetorical devices that legal writers should use less or not at all, with an explanation of why for each.

But Top 10 (or 40) lists seem to fall near the top of many lawyers' lists of things that they can't get enough of. So, to begin the book, I have broken out 50 of the adjectives and adverbs that, in my experience, legal writers use most frequently and that are likely to work against successful advocacy by distracting, confusing, annoying, or undermining the trust of their audience.

The complete Top 50 to Avoid list, without the explanations, also appears at the end of the Bonus Material section, which contains several lists of additional adjectives and adverbs that legal writers should use less often or not at all.

1. **Absolute, absolutely.** Is the thing that you're writing about really so certain? Does it admit of no exception or counterpoint? If so, feel free to use these words to convey their proper meanings. But don't use "absolutely" as just another synonym for "utterly" or "totally." And, while we're at it, don't use "utterly."

2. **Absurd, absurdly.** Some arguments do defy all common sense and are so illogical that it is laughable. But, when confronted with such a losing argument, does it really make a difference that you label it "absurd"? Are you more likely to prevail? And, too often, legal writers use these terms to describe opposing arguments or positions just because they do not like or strongly disagree with them. That use of the words is not itself absurd, but it's not helpful.

3. **Actual, actually.** These terms are properly used to distinguish something from a counterfeit or pretender or from what was expected or intended but did not happen or does not exist—such as an "actual plan." Best not to pepper this adjective into your writing if drawing that distinction isn't necessary—that is, if the "actual" thing is not different from the thing itself.

4. **Adequate, adequately.** On the one hand, if legal writing should tend toward understatement, it's hard to quibble with saying something is satisfactory or good enough. But, on the other, these words are often used to damn with faint praise or to assert that an opponent hasn't met a measure that the writer would never admit that they satisfied in any event.

5. **Almost.** A weasel word that runs rampant in legal writing. Whatever this modifies—"never," "everyone," "ran into"—will almost always be made vaguer and less precise by the pairing. (Not very satisfying, is it?) Be more precise when you can.

6. **Always.** Of how many things can you confidently say that something is true in every instance, without exception? There may be some things—you needn't always avoid "always." But to avoid overstatement and unnecessarily promising a judge what you may not be able to deliver, reserve this word for instances that leave no doubt. And avoid using the word in the less formal sense of signaling a fallback option, as in "if the Court denies the motion to dismiss, the defendant can always move for summary judgment." That's an extra word that your formal legal writing can do without every time.

7. **Apparent, apparently.** Thanks to years of thinly veiled sarcasm, these terms now tell the court that the writer doubts that what they're describing (an opponent's belief, a lawyer's reasoning) is real or true or sincere. Using these words to convey their proper meanings—that something is obvious or clearly true or is likely the case—appears (really) to be headed the way of the dodo and the literal definition of "literally."

8. **Arbitrary, arbitrarily.** Outside of the adjective's required use as part of the two-part legal term of art "arbitrary and capricious," these words' primary function in legal writing is to insult your opponent or a judge who you believe acted in a random way or based on personal whim. You could just say those things outright about the decision or action that you're describing (and criticizing). If it's true, stating it plainly would have the virtue of candor. If it's not, don't give in to the temptation to use these words to cloak an unwarranted attack.

9. **Baseless, baselessly.** These terms don't mean that a claim is wrong or offensive or not to your liking. Lawyers' accusing their opponents of making claims or assertions without any supporting facts or proof too often provides nothing but a good example of a claim or assertion without support or a basis in fact.

10. **Blatant, blatantly.** These words are usually followed by "attempt," "disregard," "falsehood," or "clear." And they are almost never necessary. If something is, for example, so clear that it cannot be missed, you can trust the judge to see it and can rest assured that saying "it is clear that X" or, better yet, just "X" will get the job done.

11. **Certainly.** In legal writing, using this term often reflects misplaced confidence. Or, in writers' more self-aware moments, it's qualified by "almost." Which unhelpfully infuses doubt into what the writer should be conveying is beyond it.

12. **Clear, clearly.** Courts and legislatures have made "clear" and "clearly" a part of many standards, including "clear error," "clear and convincing evidence," "clearly established rights," and "clearly established law." Judges unavoidably read enough uses of "clear"—often in standards that are anything but—without lawyers' piling on with tales of opponents who "clearly failed" to satisfy a governing standard or meet a legal burden or who violated a "clear requirement" of an agreement.

13. **Complete, completely.** Each of these words is an all-star of redundancy and unhelpful emphasis. The adverb is sometimes joined with "devoid" to tell the reader that something is entirely lacking or absent. Other times, it's paired with "pointless" to, I suppose, distinguish the situation in which one might say "she does sort of have a point." Sometimes, "completely" is matched up with "circular" to alert the reader that you're not talking about a not-entirely-round circle (which is, I guess, a noncircular ellipse) or an argument that only kind of assumes the conclusion to be proved. And "complete nonsense" begs the question what being a little bit nonsensical looks like and why any court would need to concern itself with the distinction.

14. **Critical, critically.** Let me pull back a curtain for you a bit: Taking the bench on a trial court gives you a new appreciation for the meaning of a false sense of urgency. Legal writers rarely use these words to describe what some lawyers do a fair bit of—express criticism or disapproval. But these terms often accompany desperate missives about something's importance or worries about timing. And yet saying it doesn't make it so. So here's a second tip: The ratio of adjectives to facts is inversely proportional to the odds that a judge is likely to put on whether she's hearing about a real emergency.

15. **Demonstrable, demonstrably.** These terms are most often followed by "false" or "incorrect" or "wrong" or "error." This is like telling the court "I will now demonstrate" and then either doing so—or not. Lawyers are not stage magicians. Lose the verbiage.

16. **Egregious, egregiously.** I'd hazard a guess that no one was ever found guilty or liable or was ever sanctioned for really base or offensive and noticeable conduct because the prosecutor, plaintiff, or opposing counsel described it with these fancy terms. Bad facts may make bad law, but they definitely make big words unnecessary.

17. **Excessive, excessively.** Outside of the contexts of "force" or "bail" or "damages," these terms aren't usually a welcome sight to a judge as they tend to be used when writers are complaining about their opponents doing or saying more than is necessary or reasonable. As with a good thing (although these words are not that), there really is such a thing as too much "too much."

18. **False, falsely, fraudulent, fraudulently.** These words are not synonyms for "wrong" or "incorrect" or "mistaken," but legal writers too often describe their opponents' factual or

even legal positions as "false" or "fraudulent" only because they disagree with them.

19.   **Frivolous, frivolously.** For too many lawyers, the adjective is a synonym for "meritless." Calling out something as frivolous is serious business. Reserve each of these words for when you mean it and can back it up.

20.   **General, generally.** These terms tell your reader that something occurs or is true more often than occasionally or even more regularly than sometimes and certainly more frequently than rarely, but less often than always or mostly, and maybe (or maybe not) at about the same rate as what is typical, regular, usual, or common. In other words, they don't tell the court much.

21.   **Genuine, genuinely.** Litigators should get their fill of these terms in the summary judgment context. These words are helpful if there's some question whether something is what it purports to be—that is, whether it is what evidence doctrines (and the English language) call "authentic." But, when used to emphasize that, or question whether, something is real or true (think "a genuine improvement"), these words often amount to unhelpful noise.

22.   **Gross, grossly.** These words are mostly used to exaggerate or mischaracterize how much something is exaggerated or mischaracterized. They're also deployed to tell the reader that someone overestimated or underestimated or miscalculated something. By how much? A gross amount—whatever that means. Leave these terms alone unless a judicial or statutory standard requires you to use them.

23.   **Groundless, groundlessly.** These are second-level lawyer insults, showing up when the writer is running out of words

to tell the court that he has the better arguments and that it should reject his opponent's position. But, when you use these terms where your opponent has some reason or evidence on her side but you just still think you should win, your deploying these words will only remind your reader of their true meanings.

24. **Incredible, incredibly.** Two words that legal writers manage to overuse both positively and negatively, describing as impossible to believe things that hardly compare to, say, a large spaceship appearing in the night sky or winning the lottery and describing as difficult to believe arguments or positions that they just don't like or want to credit.

25. **Indeed.** Are you a monocled, nineteenth-century English detective? If you use this word more often than very rarely, you risk sounding like one.

26. **Indisputable, indisputably, undisputed, undisputedly.** There aren't too many things, in the context of lawsuits, that you'll be writing about that are not contested or cannot be debated or questioned or argued about. Before you use one of these terms, make sure that you have one such unicorn as your subject.

27. **Literal, literally.** If you're using these words and not writing about the original or usual meaning of a word or distinguishing something as factually true or being what it seems to be, you're literally doing it wrong. If someone was "literally blown away," there had better have been a strong wind. (Side note: You'd better not use "had better" either.)

28. **Many.** A word that we all use all the time when we talk. But it's so indefinite (by definition) that writers feel compelled to tack on "good"—as if that helps to tell your audience how

large a thing you're talking about—or "great"—apparently to let your reader know that you're talking about more than a "good many." A good rule of thumb: Don't use "many" too many times. (Or, perhaps, don't use too many "manies"?)

29.   **Mere, merely.** When used by lawyers, the adjective is almost always followed by "fact." And it's not always a bad way to make the point as an alternative to "that fact alone" or "that fact, without more." But it's worth asking yourself how often you need to be saying to a court—even through a little, four-letter word—that something is "nothing more than" or, with the "-ly" attached (and all the negativity that comes with it), that someone is doing "nothing more than" something (saying, stating, asserting). The language offers stronger ways to convey the limits of what something is or what your opponent can do.

30.   **Meritless, meritlessly.** In a kind of moral sense, these words read like you're trying (too hard) to pull your punch while calling someone or something worthless or unworthy. In the legal sense, these terms offer a one-word way to deliver to the judge the surprising news that you don't think the other side's argument or position is a winner.

31.   **Mistaken, mistakenly.** Everyone makes mistakes. You turn left when you intended to (or the correct directions called for you to) turn right. Or you use baking soda instead of baking powder. If you're talking about one of those instances, there's no issue with using these terms. But your opponent probably isn't taking the position contrary to yours on a legal issue by mistake. If you're saying an opponent's position or argument is incorrect, just say that, or that their position or argument is "not correct." That is, in any event, less inflammatory than "mistaken," "erroneous," "misguided," or "false" and keeps the focus on the argument and not the party or lawyer advancing it.

32. **Necessary, necessarily.** These words show up in legal writing more often in the sense of inevitable than in the sense of needed or required. But an attorney's wishing something to be so is not necessarily the same as being certain that it is.

33. **Needless, needlessly.** Some requests for relief from a court or expenses in lawsuits are unnecessary because they could have been avoided. But, too often when judges see motions or costs described in these terms, they were avoidable only if the writer's opponent had given up or given in. And that use of these terms is unnecessary and best avoided.

34. **Never.** It is dangerous to speak in absolutes, and judges are naturally suspicious of what sounds like it could be an overstatement. In other instances, legal writers deploy "never" or "always" only to then diminish its reference to an absolute by working in a condition or exception in the same sentence. Avoid saying more than you need to.

35. **Obvious, obviously.** These terms are often preceded by "plainly," "rather," or "reasonably" or followed by "false," "meritless," "ridiculous," or "lie." And to no good effect, because the court doesn't need help from an adjective or adverb to see something that it couldn't miss; won't be assisted by empty assurances when trying to see or understand something that's neither clear nor apparent; and gains little from reading that "it is obvious that"—as code for "I believe that"—"my opponent [will not do something/doesn't want to actually do something it should]."

36. **Ostensible, ostensibly.** Lawyers can be a suspicious lot, and some of their clients are no less distrustful. It's no wonder they favor these terms to describe their opponent's stating or displaying one goal or motivation and secretly entertaining another. But courts try not to harbor so much mistrust,

which can lead to a disconnect that's off-putting to your audience when you give in to the impulse to use these words.

37.   **Particularly.** This term often precedes "telling" or "damning," and almost always adds nothing. Something tells in a way that matters, or it doesn't. And, however many circles Dante may have seen, there aren't really degrees of being damned, at least as far as legal rhetoric is concerned.

38.   **Plain, plainly.** Lawyers ought to feel that they write enough about these terms in connection with "error," "language," "meaning," and "text." Judges do. And, as your readers, they should be trusted to see the obvious without encountering yet another instance of one of these terms.

39.   **Rather.** The quintessential weasel word. How is being rather obvious different from being obvious? This word adds some charm on the British stage, but leave it out of your legal writing.

40.   **Readily.** Judges encounter this adverb when a legal standard requires a court to evaluate the facts against four factors and the lawyer arguing that the standard is met writes: "This factor is readily satisfied here." But, with or without that declaration, the lawyer still needs to explain how—and, unless there's credit being awarded for ease of completion, he should just get to doing that. Don't start an endzone dance before you've even scored.

41.   **Really.** This word is a versatile tool in verbal communication but is also Exhibit A that what works with the spoken word doesn't always transfer well to formal legal writing. The court doesn't need to be told that you're trying to describe reality or that your client is a really nice person. And, just as you

wouldn't write "Are you kidding me?" (or any more profane alternative phrases) in a brief, throwing in a "Really?" will just cause your reader to throw that reaction right back at you.

42. **Remarkable, remarkably.** These terms are used either to inform the court that you were really struck by first learning the facts that you're about to share or just to tell a judge to pay attention because what's coming next is worthy of her attention. A much more stylish alternative to "now hear this" or "of particular note," but no more useful.

43. **Seeming, seemingly.** What you write: "Plaintiffs offer a seemingly repentant explanation for their conduct." What a judge hears in her head: "But they're lying!" Using these apparently subtle terms may not achieve the toned-down effect that you're hoping for.

44. **Serious, seriously.** These terms generally describe a lot about litigation and the law, which involve a lot of thought and work on important matters involving difficult or challenging issues. The issue isn't that these words say the wrong thing about what they're describing. It's that they both tell a judge little that she doesn't already realize and may imply something odd and likely untrue of every other issue, consequence, or work in a matter or case—that is, that they're not important, significant, or difficult.

45. **Simply.** Asking lawyers to stop tacking this word onto "no" (as in "no evidence," "no proof," "no basis," or "no reason"), "not," "because," or "asserts" feels like a hopeless request. But hope springs eternal for optimists like me, and so I will. And, in any event, just know that this term never offers anything more than a rhetorical flourish.

46. **Supposed, supposedly.** If you find you've already used "alleged" or "allegedly" too many times, these words can be tempting substitutes. But these terms bring along the double fault of sounding more accusatory—more like you're saying that something's a lie or at least that its truth is in doubt—and carrying a less precise meaning. And, really, how many times in one brief do you need to describe something as claimed but not proven to be so?

47. **Total, totally.** These words have no place in any legal writing that isn't describing a physical structure or object that is or was completely destroyed. The adverb otherwise adds nothing by the space taken up by seven extra letters and an extra space. A judge reading, for example, that you agree or disagree with a position or that an argument lacks merit isn't left wondering if you agree or disagree only as to part of the position or think there is merit to some part of the argument—she will assume that you'd tell her if that were the case. So telling a reader that you "totally disagree" with something or that something is "totally meritless" adds nothing to the equation.

48. **Undoubted, undoubtedly.** Lawyers are often confident that their opponent undoubtedly knows or knew something. But the judge is likely to be skeptical of your ability to read minds or channel a nineteenth-century London super-sleuth.

49. **Very.** It looks innocent enough, right? It's just a little, four-letter word. And it sounds more elegant than "really, really" or "a whole lot" (by more than a lot). But that's what this term—perhaps the worst offender in a legal writer's toolbox of intensifiers and exaggerators—brings to the table: Unspecified high degrees of things or traits ("he was very excited") and unnecessary emphasis that modifies an adjective while adding no additional meaning ("it arrived the very next day").

50. **Wholly.** If it matters in context to contrast something being, for example, denied in whole from something that is being denied only in part, this word can do some good work. Otherwise, this filler word functions like unnecessary underlining or boldface on a word for emphasis ("plaintiff has wholly failed to make the required showing"). You could call it undue overemphasis. Or, better yet, don't ever use that phrase either.

More Words & Phrases to Use Less or Not at All

The language and lawyers' use of it offer more than 50 words that legal writers should avoid as much as possible or, in some instances, entirely, so here I offer, in a dictionary's style, a list of many more adjectives and adverbs, along with some other terms, phrases, and rhetorical devices. And I include with each an explanation of why—for the sake of avoiding wordiness, obscurity, overstatement, ambiguity, weasel words, incivility, or just sounding bad—legal writers should edit these words out of their motions and briefs.

A.

Abashed, abashedly. These words aren't seen too often—the opposite words "unabashed" and "unabashedly" are more commonly used in modern writing. And, if you describe someone as "abashed," you'll just cause your reader to stop and try to remember which word means "embarrassed." Just say "embarrassed" or—if it's really warranted—"ashamed."

Abated, abating. Legal writers, including maybe most often judges, use these words to say that a deadline or requirement or even an entire case is suspended or stayed. We probably should just say that.

Aberrant, aberrantly. The words of choice when a legal writer confronts a circumstance in which describing something as "abnormal" or even "not normal" or—in other contexts—"not right" or just plain "wrong" is too straightforward. Which is an aberrant circumstance indeed.

Abhorrent, abhorrently. These words might be appropriate when something, some act or statement, is so bad that no other term will do it justice. Otherwise, "awful" or "terrible" will work with less verbosity.

Abject, abjectly. These terms are commonly deployed to describe someone's disregard and, most often, failure. Used in this sense, they mean "very bad or severe." And they add nothing. Your opponent either did or did not disregard, or did or did not fail to accomplish, something. Throwing one of these words in only signals that you want to ramp up some unwelcome drama.

Abjuratory, abjured, abjuring. These words are used to gussy up a description of renouncing, repudiating, or retracting something like a position or an oath. They're useful when those words are just too simple.

Able, ably. I'm reluctant to advise anyone not to pay an opponent or colleague a compliment. And that's almost always how these words appear: "As our codefendant has ably explained,..." But this rarely adds anything because imitation—or, in legal writing, favorable quotation or citation—is already the highest form of flattery. And, when used to describe opposing counsel, sometimes accompanied by "with due respect," these terms signal no real flattery at all and should be left on the cutting-room floor.

Abnegated, abnegating. Would it be easier just to say "denied," "surrendered," or even "relinquished" or "renounced"? It would be easier on your reader. No one is paying you an extra nickel for throwing these words in.

Abnormal, abnormally. These are useful words when the reader understands the baseline for what's normal. But, otherwise, it's unhelpful to describe something as "abnormal" or "abnormally" just because you don't like it or wish it were different.

Abolished, abolishing. This sounds so lawyerly, and not in a good way. And using these words will likely conjure up in your reader's mind, at least subconsciously, some of these terms' most common objects—slavery and the death penalty. The problem is that the closest alternatives are all lawyerly, too: "abrogate," "annul," "invalidate," "negate," "nullify." Try to use any version of "abolish" and its ilk as little as you can and no more than you must.

Aborted. Why risk unconsciously distracting your reader by using this word and trying to ignore the fact that it's freighted with connotations that probably have nothing to do with what you're writing about? Go with "abandoned" or "cancelled" or "called off" or maybe even "scrapped."

Abortive, abortively. These words are not quite as freighted as "aborted" perhaps, but, still, why risk the distraction? Go with "failed" or "unsuccessful."

Abrasive, abrasively. These aren't bad words to describe something that is annoying or ill-will-inducing. But think twice about using them, regardless of whether they describe your or your client's reactions or feelings about something. Even if you're litigating about possible misconduct, legal writing is most persuasive when describing the objective or perceptible and not whether you dislike or are perturbed by something or someone.

Abrogated, abrogating. These terms belong near the top of any list of words that only lawyers use. And sometimes they may be the most accurate way to describe, for example, how a statute or common law has officially been ended. But there's usually an alternative that will make your writing flow better with simpler prose—a statute may have been repealed, a rule revoked, or a common-law doctrine invalidated or limited.

Abrupt, abruptly. How often do you really need, in legal writing, to describe the way that something stopped or changed? If it matters that something came to a stop suddenly and unexpectedly, as opposed to gradually and as expected, these terms are useful for drawing that distinction. Otherwise, they commonly serve as filler or, worse, unnecessarily turn up the heat in a writer's rhetoric.

Absorbed, absorbedly. These words are more often used with "self-" in front of them. And that's a thought about an opponent, client, or judge that a legal writer best keeps to himself.

Abstemious, abstemiously. This adjective means "not self-indulgent." Which cannot be said of any writer using these five-dollar words.

Abstract, abstractly. These terms appear in legal writing to describe how an opponent's argument or an unfavorable reading of a statute or rule could apply to some hypothetical situation—usually accompanied by assurances that that theoretical possibility can be confined to a Picassoesque alternate reality never seen in real life.

Abstruse, abstrusely. These words should not be confused with "obtuse." Although that might be a good word to describe or explain a choice to burden your reader with "abstruse." Both are obscure words and difficult to understand—although, as your reader will find (when forced to check the dictionary), this particular obscure and difficult-to-understand adjective means "obscure" or "difficult to understand."

Abundant, abundantly. This adverb is almost always followed by "clear." It's difficult to imagine when it would matter that something was not just clear but—assuming there even is a difference—abundantly clear. If you have discovered such an instance, maybe you should leave in "abundantly." Otherwise, "clear"—or whatever other adjective might follow this overused adverb—should be allowed to do its work unadorned.

Accidental, accidentally. The worry with these words for legal writers is that they can be misused as weasel words—that is, a word used to qualify or make ambiguous an otherwise straightforward or direct statement.

Accurate, accurately. This adjective is often preceded by "not exactly" or "not entirely," to more politely say that the judge or an opponent got some details or facts wrong.

Acerbic, acerbically. You shouldn't be using "harsh" or "severe" so much in your writing that you need to reach for these fancy words to mix things up. Also, if a judge reads "acerbically" too quickly, it looks like "aerobically." Which is not, I'm guessing, what you mean to convey. Lose this adverb, and avoid that likely distraction and possible confusion.

Acrid, acridly. These may be the best words to describe certain smells, odors, stenches, fumes, or smoke. In any other context, find another way to say that you find anything else distasteful or offensive.

Active, actively. Occasionally legal writers need to contrast someone's role in some effort or activity with a more passive counterpart or alternative. More often, these terms show up in briefs with "undermine," "deceive," "mislead," or another verb describing conduct that is hardly static, as a sort of aside or verbal version of bolded underlining to tell a judge that "he really is doing this." Actively resist the urge to do that.

Ad hoc. Because living writers shouldn't need to use a dead language, we should have a better English alternative to this Latin phrase meaning "for this." You can and should use "as-needed" as needed, whenever possible. But, otherwise, we're stuck with "special purpose," or "special committee," which not even corporate boards enjoy.

Ad hominem. This is most likely used to describe how opposing counsel is personally attacking the writer. In that context, attaching this label to what is happening may not be more off-putting—even accounting for the Latin—than saying "personal attacks," "character assaults," or (most overused and usually overwrought) "character assassination." But, if it occurs in briefing or argument before the court, a judge will recognize this kind of thing without your describing it or pointing it out. And, as a general matter, do your legal writing in (plain) English, not Latin.

Ad nauseam. This phrase is, properly understood, an insult. Avoid trafficking in insults, even in foreign or dead languages.

Adamant, adamantly. These terms are used to let the reader know that the opposition to something is strong. Really strong. Rock hard. As unyielding as steel—or adamantium. Important to include in any situation in which the judge or other decisionmaker will give the win to the side who feels most strongly that their opponent is wrong.

Additional, additionally. To avoid another "another," this adjective will sometimes do. But both the adjective and the adverb can also read like "and another thing," and without any additional charm.

Addled. I like the way this word sounds. But don't use it to describe your opponent or a judge. Really, you can only use this in legal writing to describe what happened to someone as a matter of historical fact—and, even then, it's probably better just to say that someone became confused.

Adjunct, adjunctly. This adjective refers to a law school instructor who has another day job. Don't bother trying to make it mean something else.

Aforementioned. This word may be useful because it does the work of several words in a single word. But it's so stilted. For the sake of making your writing sound like you speak (when you speak well), use "described above" or "mentioned earlier" instead.

Aggravated, aggravatedly, aggravating, aggravatingly. These adjectives play a big role in criminal law terms of art. But using them outside of this context not only tells a court that you're annoyed but also that you're angry about it—and doing so using terms that also describe particularly violent robberies and assaults.

Aggressive, aggressively. Outside of describing an assault, these terms often pretty well capture a writer's use of them to describe others' arguments or positions.

Agonizing, agonizingly. These are legal writers' words of choice for exaggerating fairly run-of-the-mill choices or problems.

Aimless, aimlessly. These can be good words when they're called for, but bear in mind that all who wander aren't directionless or purposeless.

Alarming, alarmingly. These are often used to describe opposing counsel's actions or inaction—and pretty much always to report something other than someone's pulse or heart rate being extremely low. Better just to describe the facts and let the judge become alarmed.

Amazing, amazingly. You may be describing an event that surprised or astonished someone, and maybe this adjective or adverb enhances the tale's telling. But, if you're tempted in legal writing to use these words to convey that something is really good or cool, you should spare your reader what will often smack of snark or an homage to your favorite comic books.

Ambiguous, ambiguously. These terms get so much airplay with statutes, contracts, and rules. Judges don't need to hear them on other channels.

Ambivalent, ambivalently. These terms are really up in the (mixed) feelings of the writer. And they describe a kind of conflict that's probably best kept to yourself.

Ample, amply. These words often accompany "demonstrate" to let the court know that the writer has shown not just enough but more than enough. Which is important any time that extra credit is being awarded.

Amplified. This sounds like a loud guitar riff coming out of a big pair of speakers. Choose a different tune.

Analogous, analogously. Telling your reader that you're using an analogy is a bit self-referential and stilted. It's kind of like telling your audience that you're going to describe something before just doing it.

Annoyed, annoyedly, annoying, annoyingly. If you're using any of these words, it is always about you. It's probably not legally important that something triggers you, so just describe how your opponent is or isn't behaving.

Antiquated, antiquatedly. These terms are pretty much limited these days to describing a class of notions or rules. And, like some of their synonyms, they offer the quaint charm of serving as fine examples of their own meanings.

Antithetical, antithetically. However hard "plain language" may be to exactly define, these words are the opposite of it.

Apocryphal, apocryphally. For Catholic readers, these words might call more to mind than you intend. And too many others may struggle to recall if these terms mean really old and outdated or well-known but unverifiable. Avoid that risk and pack more of a punch by describing a tale or quote as "unverified" or "likely not authentic" or "improbable."

Appalling, appalled, appallingly. If the conduct or statement in question really is worthy of one of these labels, describe it, and let the court come to that conclusion on its own.

Approximate, approximately. These words sound more formal than "roughly" and more exact or precise than "almost" or "around." But, when used too often, they sound like hedging.

Apt, aptly. These most often appear as a compliment to someone who named some doctrine or place. Which is probably a nice sentiment but unlikely to be important to the matter at hand.

Arcane, arcanely. These terms conjure up images of dark secrets and ancient magic. Which, unless you're litigating a case about role-playing games or ancient druids, probably isn't what you're going for.

Archaic, archaically. This is another pair of words that fit their own meanings. Save them for the historians and paleontologists. Just say "old" or "outdated."

Arguendo. Assume, for the sake of argument, that your reader can understand from context what you mean by "assuming" some facts that you don't like or might not agree are true. No Latin necessary.

Argumentative, argumentatively. Outside of an objection to a question to a witness in court, this word describes someone as enjoying or being prone to making arguments. The court doesn't need you to tell it that your opponent is making many or frequent arguments—and, in any event, a judge won't be surprised to hear this said of a lawyer or litigant.

Arrogant, arrogantly. Each of these words should stay a quiet thing that you never say out loud. If it's true, the judge will see it for herself in your opponent's behavior.

Artful, artfully. To modern ears, these terms sound more flattering than the cunning or deceitful manner that their proper meanings often convey. Confine your rhetorical flair to less slippery turns of phrase.

Ashamed. Someone who is involved in a fact pattern before the court may have felt shame, and this is a good word for describing that. But, when a legal writer uses this adjective to describe how an opponent or a judge feels or probably feels or (more often) should feel, something has gone amiss.

Ashamedly. This adverb is almost always directed at an opponent or a court and describes not how the writer knows that the opponent or the court feels but rather how the writer believes the opposing party or counsel or a judge should feel. Don't use this clunky word to try to say indirectly what you wouldn't write directly as "For shame!" or "Have you no shame?"

Asinine, asininely. It's not helpful to describe your opponent's argument or a court's reasoning as foolish, unintelligent, silly, or stupid, and using one of these words—which originate from a Latin term meaning "like an ass or donkey"—to convey that meaning only makes it worse.

Assert, contend, argue. Don't tell the judge that you're telling the judge—just say it directly. And, if you're describing the other side's positions, mix it up. But don't ever say that a judge "contends" or "asserts."

Assiduous, assiduously. A fancy way of saying "really really." And, if you wouldn't write that phrase in a brief, don't resort to one of these spelling-bee words as a backup.

Astonishing, astonishingly. Will the judge be astonished? How would you know? Are, or were, you filled with sudden surprise or wonder? Please take this the right way: Who cares? Leave these words on the shelf unless you have a set of facts in which describing someone's reaction is important in the telling.

Attenuated, attenuating. The fancy cousins of "lessened," "reduced," and "weakened." And no stronger for the extra flashiness.

Awful. You don't need to use this adjective to describe what makes behavior terrible or a smell unpleasant. And, as an adverb, it's awful informal—you're making a legal argument, not writing a play set in the antebellum American South.

Awfully. In formal legal writing, you shouldn't need to say that something is very bad or that someone is incredibly nice or that you're extremely sorry. But you certainly don't need to say it using something that maybe isn't a real word.

Awkward, awkwardly. Sometimes saying these things out loud only makes them more true. Handle these terms with care and grace.

B.

Backward. This just comes off as mean, unless you're describing the direction that someone is walking or something is moving. And adding an *s* doesn't make it better—it just makes it British.

Baffled, baffling, bafflingly, bewildered, bewilderedly, bewildering, bewilderingly. Telling a court that someone else's argument or point is extremely confusing or is just not understandable at all feels like overdoing it. Telling a court that you're extremely confused or puzzled feels like oversharing.

Bald, baldly. These words are, more often than not, followed by some form of "assertion." "Unsupported" does a lot more work—or at least the same work without the whiff of an empty rhetorical flourish.

Bald-faced, boldfaced. These terms describe a special kind of lie. Apparently. Calling out someone as a liar in legal writing is already a bit much without layering on a beard/no-beard metaphor.

Banal, banally. Maybe Hannah Arendt ruined these words for us with her famous formulation 60 years ago, but they now sound more like a reference to something evil than something unoriginal.

Bare, barely. These terms are mostly used to describe just a teensy-weensy amount of thought or mention.

Basic, basically. Are you describing the fundamental building blocks of, for example, chemistry? If not, you're probably misusing these terms as weasel words or to insult your opponent as having a misunderstanding of something fundamental or otherwise being simple or ignorant. Or, worse, preferring all things mainstream and conventional. At best, these words operate as unnecessary filler.

Bastardized. Whatever its proper meaning, the root of this word just makes it jarring to a modern ear to hear.

Befuddled, befuddling, befuddlingly. These are such fun words. Maybe a little too fun for a legal brief.

Begrudged, begrudging, begrudgingly. These terms will often be confused with "grudgingly," but with the "be-" comes resentment or, really, envy. And, with it, a little too much amateur psychology or mind-reading for any legal brief.

Belied, belying. There's always a better approach than calling someone a liar. And adding "be-" at the front doesn't make these words land any better.

Believable, believably. Judges mostly encounter these words in a negative sense—telling the court that it shouldn't believe an argument or representation that someone else is making. The words themselves aren't usually an issue—the lack of an explanation as to why often is.

Besotted, besotting. Wow, these are so British. In American legal writing, "drunk" or "intoxicated" will work just fine.

Beyond peradventure. This is an ancient and strange phrase that should only be used as a term of art where a governing legal standard requires it.

Bitter, bitterly. Let's assume that you're not writing about food or beer. If you're not, it's a stretch to imagine when you should be conveying your or even someone else's anger or disappointment or other feelings, much less amping up the volume of your account with these terms.

Bizarre, bizarrely. A few legal standards use these terms to fill out the parameters of something that's legally frivolous. Otherwise, if someone is acting so strangely that you're tempted to tag them with these labels, you're better off fully describing their conduct or statements.

Blinding, blindingly. If you're dealing with someone with superhuman speed, go ahead and add this to "fast." Otherwise, judges see this alongside "obvious" to helpfully convey that something isn't just self-evident or apparent but so very much so that anyone who can see will know it.

Blinkered. This is kind of a fun word. But it also sounds like you're talking about your car's hazard lights.

Blissful. You're not writing a romance novel.

Blissfully. This adverb will almost always be followed by "ignorant"—or maybe "unaware." Either way, it's gratuitous sarcasm.

Bloodsucking. Unless you're describing a particularly gruesome event, this word should never make it into a final draft.

Bluff, bluffly. These words are an adjective and an adverb. No kidding. But most modern readers will think you must have poker on your mind and misplaced or misspelled the more commonly understood verb or noun forms of the words.

Blunt, bluntly. Lawyers lead off a sentence with "Bluntly" as a signal that they're about to wield a truth hammer on the opposition. There's no need to broadcast to a judge that you're about to straightforwardly and honestly describe something. And there's really no need to use the adjective to tell a court that someone is forthright and honest no matter what—unless that really matters.

Bonkers. If there's a good reason to discuss someone's mental stability in a legal writing, you need to do so a bit more delicately or clinically than this.

Boundless, boundlessly. If someone's energy or ambition truly knows no bounds, these terms offer some economy in saying so. But most human beings have, you know, human limits, and so these terms almost always carry a tinge of exaggeration that doesn't serve you well.

Brassbound. Did you know that this is an adjective that can mean rigid, inflexible, impudent, or brazen? If you used it in a first draft and you're now checking on it, maybe you did. But most readers won't.

Brazen, brazenly. If you're not using these words to describe some outlandish behavior on a beach somewhere, you're probably just signaling to your reader your shock and dismay that your opponent dares to defy your arguments.

Breathless, breathlessly. These terms are usually used to characterize how an opponent is making an argument. But using these words won't take your reader's breath away. Certainly not in a good way.

Brilliant, brilliantly. These terms too often appear as another weaponized superlative, conscripted into the service of a back-handed compliment.

Broad, broadly. These are very general words to convey that something covers or includes most but not all of some other things. In other words, these are generally filler words that your audience won't miss and that your writing can do without.

Broad-ranging, wide-ranging. These are the words of choice to complain about opponents' discovery efforts or a government inquiry without really telling the court just how far over the line they've gone in coverage or scope.

Bullish, bullishly. If you can bear the financial overtones of these terms, they can be useful and nuanced alternatives to "hopeful," "confident," and "optimistic."

C.

Cagey, cagily. This adjective sounds like it means being trapped, but it actually refers to someone's avoiding (at least figuratively) just that. And the adverb sounds more like the name of an exotic tropical fish or big cat.

Capricious, capriciously. This adjective is almost never used without being preceded by "arbitrary and." And, at least in that pairing, legal writers and analysis rarely seem to give any effect to this tag-along adjective's independent meaning: impulsive or sudden. If that's what you mean, go with one of those words instead, and reserve these fancier terms for that two-part term of art when a governing legal standard forces you to use it.

Cautious, cautiously. These terms are apparently required qualifiers for any almost any lawyer's expression of optimism.

Cavalier, cavalierly. Why say someone "is not taking this seriously" when you can call upon allusions to an English civil war almost 400 years ago? Perhaps we should just be grateful that the nickname for the other side of that conflict didn't catch on in a broader context. Roundheadedly, indeed.

Ceaseless, ceaselessly. Whatever it is that you're describing, it's almost certainly not actually endless. And you're probably not celebrating whatever this thing is that's supposedly without end. In any event, the court's patience for overly critical exaggeration almost certainly isn't unending.

Chaotic, chaotically. These words are more likely to call to mind role-playing characters than scenes of confusion or disorder.

Charitable, charitably. Outside of the tax code, courts see these terms attached to some variation of "description" and, too often, as conveying anything but kindness or mercy.

Chary, charily. Words that look and sound like they describe a stone fruit that's on guard against lurking threats.

Cheeky, cheekily. However playful you feel you can occasionally be in a brief, these British terms are out of bounds.

Churlish, churlishly. Whatever the wisdom (or lack thereof) of calling an opponent rude, you're showing your reader no courtesies when using a term with a definition that requires references to "boorish" and "surly" to describe its bounds.

Circular, circularly. These terms are most often deployed with "reasoning" or "argument" to attack an opponent's logic. But, as with irony, efforts to call out this fallacy in practice generally aren't worth the price of admission. If it's true, you're less likely to get tied up in knots if you just say that an argument's premises assume its conclusion.

Civil, civilly. These words too often describe only the relations and conduct of lawyers in the criminal bar and not the practice within the namesake counterpart. But, by all means, use these terms in writing any time that you can in service of working to change that.

Clever, cleverest, cleverly. These terms appear in legal writing most often as backhanded compliments, and usually without much wit or ingenuity.

Clumsy, clumsily. These words offer an apt description of some legal procedures and mechanisms but deliver a bit too much of an insult when applied to your fellow lawyers and their efforts.

Coincident, coincidental, coincidentally. In much legal writing, there apparently are no coincidences—only thinly veiled, sarcastic references to what must actually be a conspiracy or coverup.

Colorful, colorfully. These terms more often describe "language" and not "characters" in legal writing. At times the euphemism may be welcome, but usually you can just say "profane" and leave no more than need be to your reader's imagination.

Colossal. This term often seems to describe a really big mistake. But describing something as a mistake in legal writing is a big deal regardless. Think hard about whether you need this intensifier.

Colossally. This word is pretty much always followed by "stupid." And, so, it's pretty much never a good idea to use this in legal writing.

Commonly. Your mind probably filled in "referred to" as you read this word. And a judge reading your brief is likely to do so as well, regardless of the context in which you're using it.

Compelling, compellingly. On the one hand, there are only so many times you should write "convincing" or "persuasive," and so an alternative may be needed. On the other, there are only so many times—fewer than you might think—that you should be telling a court that or how it should be swayed by a point or argument rather than making your case and letting the court get there on its own.

Competent, competently. That's not saying much for someone or something, is it? You should be able to do better—or say nothing at all—unless a legal standard requires you to handle these terms.

Complicated, complicatedly, complicating. These words very well describe people and life in general. But, assuming you're more likely describing an issue or argument, think twice about whether you need to characterize it at all at this level.

Compunctious. This adjective screams "this is a big word that you may not know the meaning of and likely will confuse with another similar sounding big word." Use "regretful" or "remorseful" or "contrite" or really anything else to convey what you mean.

Conceivable, conceivably. It's hard to imagine a much lower bar than these terms describe something as clearing. Maybe some legal standards require nothing more and, so, make this a point worth saying. Anything's possible, I suppose.

Concerning, concerningly. This adjective means to cause or induce worry or concern or disquiet. A good word if "worrisome" or "troubling" won't work—but just be aware that some readers may stumble over its use outside its most common usage as a preposition.

Conclusory. Some dictionaries will tell you that this is just a synonym for "conclusive." But anyone litigating cases in American courts in the last few decades knows it better as an overused word to describe an unsupported conclusion or assertion. It may at one time have been a fair charge that this isn't a real word, but there's no putting that genie back in the bottle. Just don't rub the lamp any more than you really must—or take the leap to "conclusorily," which isn't a real word (or at least shouldn't be).

Concomitant, concomitantly. Using "accompanying," "associated," or even "attendant" instead will bring with it much-appreciated immediate comprehension for your reader.

Concrete, concretely. These terms are helpful for those times when "specific," "particular," or "real" just don't do enough to conjure images or feelings of building materials.

Concurrent, concurrently. In my experience, when reading these terms, lawyers and judges often must pause to ask themselves, "Does this mean at the same time or one after the other?" That gets old after the first time, and it isn't made better by stringing together repeated instances of that experience. Some legal standards demand that you use these words as terms of art, but, otherwise, give everyone a break, and spell it out in plain terms.

Condescending, condescendingly. Unfortunately, the law is not the place to go to avoid anyone with a patronizing or superior attitude. But the best way to respond in writing isn't to slap this label on them. Be gracious; let it go unmentioned. And, if an attorney's or party's attitude comes out enough, trust that the judge will notice it herself.

Confounded, confoundedly, confounding, confoundingly. These terms sound like you considered "confused" but thought "I'd like my reader to experience a little bit of that feeling herself, so let me grab my thesaurus."

Confused, confusedly, confusing, confusingly. These are useful terms for an all-too-common state of affairs for all of us. But they play better when directed at yourself than your opponent.

Conjectural, conjecturally. Sticking with "speculative" avoids these terms that each sound a bit like you're just making up the word as you go along by stringing together syllables chosen at random.

Conscious, consciously. These terms always seem to be followed by "choice" or "chose." Which may at first seem redundant—until you consider some of the reflexive decisions you may have seen or made. Still, no need to use these terms to draw the contrast unless you need to stave off a "just didn't give it much thought" claim.

Consequent, consequently, consequential, consequentially. A rare example in which the adverbs are more palatable than the adjectives. And, while you should go with "resulting" instead when an adjective is called for, these adverbs still get the nod over the more awful "resultingly" or "resultantly."

Conservative, conservatively. In the beginning, these terms had nonpolitical meanings. But now, it seems, they hardly do. Take the cautious route of finding an alternative.

Conspicuous, conspicuously. These terms are almost always followed by "absence" or "absent" or "leaves out" and then naturally raise the question why you need to point out the obvious.

Constant, constantly. Some therapists and interpersonal communication specialists advise that you shouldn't couch complaints in absolute terms, accusing someone of "always" doing or saying something when, in fact, of course they're not. These terms feel like the legal writing equivalent.

Constructive, constructively. The law has a lot of uses for these terms. And, however longwinded it may be, "constructive criticism" is neither going away nor taxing any reader's comprehension. But otherwise these terms may not serve a useful purpose when simpler alternatives are available.

Contemporaneous, contemporaneously. The alternative terms aren't much less overformal. But your writing won't suffer from just saying "during the same time period."

Contemptible, contemptibly. "Contempt" is a loaded enough term in the law. Nobody benefits from making it into an adjective or adverb.

Contemptuous, contemptuously. Hopefully you can make it through any brief without describing anyone as full of disdain, hatred, or scorn.

Contentious, contentiously. These terms are sometimes useful to label an issue or debate. But, in legal circles, this adjective can—and probably should—go without saying about any attorney you'd be inclined to describe this way.

Contingent, contingently. From fees to warrants and contracts, judges read enough of these terms that manage to make "dependent" and "conditional" sound unfussy.

Controverted, controvertible. A fine example of terms that only attorneys would use to gussy up their writing as alternatives to the very lawyerly terms "debated," "disputed," "opposed," "debatable," and "disputable."

Contumacious, contumaciously. These monstrosities signal that someone is stubbornly or deliberately disobedient. Certain legal standards have enshrined these terms' places in legal briefs and opinions in the context of the doctrines burdened by those standards. Please don't foster their further spread.

Convincing, convincingly. Legal writing doesn't usually involve parties' agreeing with one another's arguments. Judges would be a bit taken aback to read a brief that says "the movant's main argument is convincing, and we now agree to dismiss the case." Little surprise, then, that these words most often appear with a "not" in front of them—which means that the writer is telling the court how it will respond to competing lines of reasoning. Don't get out over your skis—stay in your lane, and explain why and how the judge should be swayed by your analysis. And do it without a bunch of clichés.

Cowardly. This word probably first calls to mind for readers, even across generations, a certain lion. The next reaction that most often follows is also the right one: You can't say this about another lawyer or litigant, much less a judge. Your opponent may be worthy of this title, but let the judge reading your brief reach that conclusion herself and respond accordingly.

Crafty, craftily. Like their "artful" companion, these terms sound more flattering than their suggestions of subtlety, guile, and cunning really convey. Leave the field on these words to the much less judgy decoration and architecture contexts.

Craven, cravenly. These are certainly not the most accessible terms for cowardice, but "gutless," "spineless," and "lily-livered" hardly recommend themselves for brief writing either. Take that as a cue to rise above the fray and pass on calling anyone a chicken.

Crazed, crazedly, crazy, crazily. If you're using these terms outside of a context in which you're also discussing psychosis and possibly asylums, it's time to step back from your keyboard for a bit and then dial down your rhetoric.

Credible, credibly. These terms carry a lot of water in many legal contexts. But they come off as lightweight when judges read about what an opponent "cannot credibly argue" in situations that seem to confuse "could" with "should" as to what the court might believe or accept.

Credulous, credulously. There's little to recommend these terms that make "gullible" and "naive" seem straightforward and accessible.

Crushing, crushingly. These words apparently describe a species of defeat that lives mostly in the imaginations of lawyers writing early in a case.

Curmudgeonly. This doesn't show up much in legal writing. It might in any reviews of this book.

Cursory, cursorily. After reading hundreds of briefs, an experienced judge could be forgiven for believing that this level of a review will always reveal misconduct, shenanigans, or at least grievous shortcomings by the other side of a dispute.

D.

Damning, damningly. These can be evocative terms in context, but they're perhaps a little suggestive for some readers. When venturing down this path, no need to abandon all hope, but do carefully consider your audience.

Dastardly. If you're writing a brief about characters in a melodrama or vintage cartoon, good for you—that's awesome. How fun. But, otherwise, what are you doing with this word?

Daunted, dauntedly, daunting, dauntingly, dauntless, dauntlessly, undaunted, undauntedly. You should give a miss to any word derived from "daunt," which sounds like "did" and "not" just ran out of steam when trying to form a contraction.

Deafening, deafeningly. When paired with "silence," these terms can offer an effective bit of imagery that's not easily conveyed otherwise. But, when used too often, the court may be unable to hear the eloquence.

Debatable, debatably. At least among lawyers, most things are up for debate, so these words describe a pretty low bar and may not add much to your messaging to a court.

Decent, decently. Outside of their more moral or respectable meanings, these terms offer a pretty okay way to say that something is adequate or satisfactory. Your writing deserves better.

Decimated. This adjective is often used to suggest that a position or argument has been thoroughly refuted or rebutted. But it means to randomly kill every tenth person in a group. Save it for the very rare occasion when you need to describe something approximating that kind of atrocity.

Defiant, defiantly. In a legal context, these terms' value depends on what someone is disregarding or resisting. They may be useful if it's a court order; they may sound like whining if it's a competing position or argument that your opponent is challenging.

Deficient, deficiently. As insults go, these terms don't tell your reader much unless you explain what's wanting. And that's too often missing when these words get thrown at an argument or evidence.

Definite, definitely. Less-than-careful overuse has made the meanings of these words (as used in legal writing) unclear, inexact, and without clear limits—confusing "definite" in the sense of "proof" with "definite" in the sense of a strong belief or opinion. A definite loss to the language, to be sure.

Definitive, definitively. Lawyers have been known to confuse their preferred outcome or chosen expert with the actual (often yet unknown) decisive result or answer or most authoritative source.

Deleterious, deleteriously. With eleven syllables between them, these are two words that are sure to have an injurious effect on your brief's readability. You can sound plenty smart sticking with "harmful" or "make worse."

Deliberate, deliberately. When lawyers write of their opponents' "deliberately refusing to follow the court's instructions" or "deliberate effort to confuse the issues," courts are at times left to wonder where the writer obtained this penetrating insight into the other counsel's or party's psyche. And, if there's no real suggestion that the other side may have done or failed to do something by accident, these terms tend to generate more heat than light in your briefing.

Demonic, demonically. If true, it's probably not a judge that you need. Step away from your computer, and get some real help.

Deplorable, deplorably. Sometimes, in a broader cultural context, words get placed in a basket from which they can't escape. These terms seem to fit that bill within the last decade.

Destroyed. Litigation isn't a game. But it isn't war either. Reserve this kind of terminology for the sort of violent events or conduct that this word is primarily used to describe.

Devilish, devilishly. These terms mostly seem to describe a grin. How a sly smile merits a reference to biblical figures, I couldn't tell you. And, for our purposes, you're not writing about smirking or evil spirits, are you?

Dialogue. This term is sometimes used as a substitute for "discuss." Avoid the temptation to misuse this noun as a verb. This word also describes a literary device that is sometimes used by legal writers to make a point by recounting an imagined conversation, often among judges. For example: "'Judge Johnson, have you read this argument contending that contracts must be read for plain meaning?' 'I've always thought that is a winning position, Judge Smith.' 'Me, too. I've thought through all the other possible positions, and it's hard not to go with that one.' 'Yep. I agree.' (Exchanging high fives.) '[Both:] Q.E.D.'" Some lawyers have pulled this off. But please don't try to follow that lead. A playwright, you are not.

Directly. When a court is told that something is "directly relevant" (as this term is often used), it sometimes suggests either a false comparison, because there's nothing "indirectly relevant" in play, or that the writer is confusing types of relevance with direct versus circumstantial evidence. "Directly" mostly functions as meaningless emphasis that isn't relevant or helpful to assessing the degree of relevance.

Discriminating, discriminatingly. While in some contexts these words convey something about good taste, in legal circles they likely first bring to mind acting on a prejudice.

Disdainful, disdainfully. These terms may be the poster children for the proposition that every emotion needs adjectival and adverbial companions. But they're also proof that that's apparently not true.

Disingenuous, disingenuously. You're not quite calling someone a liar—but these terms come close enough that you should hesitate to use them to call out a lawyer, party, or witness as insincere or lacking in candor.

Disjointed, disjointedly. None of these terms are nice to say, but stick with "confusing," "illogical," "disorganized," or even "incoherent."

Disparaging, disparagingly. Courts hear these terms enough in employment and trade name cases and settlements involving reputations. They can do without the "I won't disparage my opponent by [fill in the blank]" rhetorical turns (that is, apophasis or paralipsis—for those keeping track of our ancient-Greek-derived Latin references).

Disposable, disposably. These words sound like a reference to actual trash or garbage and so themselves should be consigned to the editing rubbish bin.

Dispositive, dispositively. These terms are clunky on their best days, and they get more than enough attention through some unavoidable terms of art.

Disturbed, disturbing, disturbingly. Don't reach for these terms as substitutes for "bothered" or "upset" unless you're addressing a situation that warrants the emotional or mental health overtones.

Do not bother, did not bother. These phrases offer a way to describe an omission or inaction that tells the court that you are very bothered or angry—and that does nothing to increase the likelihood that the judge will share your frustration.

Dodgy. This is a fun British word for a host of questionable or downright bad character traits. But: (1) Are you British? (2) Do you want to cause your reader to get distracted wondering if you are British? (3) If your reader knows that you're not British, do you want her to think that you're an overeager Anglophile? (4) Do you really need to describe something this way in a brief in any event?

Don't disagree. Avoid double negatives. They're muddy at best. If the fact that you don't disagree is all that you can represent to the court, so be it. But it's a poor substitute for agreement—which is a much better thing to report if you can. And telling a judge only that you don't disagree just raises the question whether you actually agree but don't want to say so for some reason or you are just neutral or indifferent and really do neither agree nor disagree.

Doubtful, doubtfully, dubious, dubiously. In legal writing, talk of doubts and disbelief only helps a judge when it's clear who's doing the doubting and disbelieving and why it matters. Otherwise, using these terms is no more persuasive than telling the court "some people don't believe" or "it may be doubted."

Downright, downrightly. If you wouldn't include "utter," "outright," or "out-and-out" in your brief (and you shouldn't), you should extend that ban to these terms as well.

Drab, drably. No one reading these terms will have anything in mind but brown paint or light brown colored clothes. And why do you want to do that to your audience?

Dreadful, dreadfully. Unless you're describing something that induces great fear or terror, using these terms makes you sound like a Brit describing typical London weather.

Dreary, drearily. You're thinking about the weather now, right? Your reader will be, too, when reading these terms, so best to save them for a rainy day.

Droll, drolly. To traditionalist wordsmiths, these terms mean oddly funny or whimsical. To some, they also describe a dry wit.

To many, these words sound like they should mean dreary and dull all at once—but they mean neither. And it'd be funny (but not in a ha-ha way) to see these terms in a brief that doesn't involve a case about a comedian.

Dull, dully. There may be no better way to describe that knife that wasn't sharp. But, if you really do need to describe someone as stupid or something as boring, just own it, and use those terms. Or, better, avoid the "stupid" label in any form.

Dumb, dumbly. If you're discussing something or someone who can't speak, go with "mute"—or just spell it out in plain terms. If you want to label someone or something as stupid or lacking intelligence, you should probably take a pause and then mimic the formal meanings of these words.

Dumbfounded, dumbfoundedly. This is a word that sounds great—in its adjective form. But you should rarely need to write to a judge that you, she, or someone else was or should be so shocked or amazed as to become speechless.

Duplicitous, duplicitously. Unless you're talking about a criminal charging instrument with multiple allegations, just say that the person is "deceitful"—or make it really simple and call them a liar. Or better yet, don't, and leave these labels for the court to employ when they're really called for.

E.

Easy, easily. This adverb is usually offered up when it doesn't matter how hard something (refuting, repudiating, disposing of) is to do—and often in the form "easily the most [some negative adjective]" when whether someone is the worst of the offenders doesn't matter to the court and the "easily" just serves as the word equivalent of "!!!"

Emphatic, emphatically. These terms are essentially an exclamation point in word form. You should, without a doubt, definitely not use them.

Endemic, endemically. You may mean to generically convey that something is widespread or prevalent, but, after 2020, your reader will be thinking about a global outbreak of a contagious disease.

Endless, endlessly. These words sound like you are complaining about something—or mixed up your draft brief with that young-adult coming-of-age screenplay that you're writing on the side.

Enigmatic, enigmatically. Whatever may be said of Sir Winston Churchill's famous statement, layering these terms on top of something that's already puzzling may only deepen the mystery for your reader—and not in a way that's fun or inviting.

Enormous, enormously. These terms are less overused than "huge" or "immense," and less silly than "ginormous" or even "gigantic," but still take up too much space when "big" or "large" or "very big" will usually do.

Entire, entirely. This adverb shows up to modify "different," where it can helpfully convey the degree of difference, or "new," where it is less helpful when something either is or is not new but, if new, may be more or less different than what went before. And the adjective shows up where it's not needed, when there's little question that something was or was not left out.

Erroneous, erroneously. At least in litigation, and particularly at the appellate stage, so much of what courts must decide depends on terms of art like "clear error," "plain error," and "reversible error" as subsets of what a court is deciding. And that is whether some action or inaction taken by a trial court was error, or erroneous. Like it or not, appellate courts have occupied the field on these terms, and it's just not helpful to hear that a lawyer did or said something "erroneously" (whether in terms of morality, truth, or judgment) without a reliable metric for what that means.

Especial, especially. This adjective offers an excellent vehicle to say that something is exceptional in a manner that is particularly likely to make your reader think you meant to say "special." On the flip side, your reader expects the e before "specially" but also—with any experience reading briefs—will expect that whatever follows isn't exceptionally likely to be unusual or outstanding.

Essential, essentially. These terms mean absolutely necessary or basic to something. You wouldn't know that from how often they show up as a more articulate version of "nice to have."

Eventful, eventfully. These terms usually function as an understatement for total chaos or pandemonium.

Evermore. Quoth not the poem nor the song title. And, so too, nevermore should "nevermore" be heard from in your legal briefing.

Evident, evidently. These are words of choice for throat-clearing ("it is evident that [something not at all obvious]") or veiled sarcasm ("my opponent evidently believes [a thing that no one could accept as true]"). If something really is obvious or unmistakable—and if and when it'll be helpful to the court to point it out—leave no doubt, and use those words instead.

Eviscerated, eviscerating. Are you removing someone's or something's inner organs? Even metaphorically? Is that the image that you're looking to plant in a judge's mind?

Exact, exactly. When a writer is not discussing measurements or numbers that aren't approximate, these terms show up as an adverb either before "same"—to assure your reader that you know what "same" means and didn't confuse it with "similar"—or after "not"—to blur the lines between "not at all" or "somewhat but not completely."

Exasperated, exasperatedly, exasperating, exasperatingly. Sometimes a court needs a writer to, while conveying some historical facts, explain that someone was very irritated and frustrated. Sometimes, but not often.

Exceeding, exceedingly. Judges know from experience that these terms often denote what the writer really wants to be the case—or, perhaps most often, hopes to be likely—and that, almost as often, they signal little more than that.

Exclamation marks. These are the written equivalent of raising your voice, or even yelling at your audience. Which is a court—and, more specifically, the judge whom you are trying to convince to adopt your position and possibly the law clerks or staff attorneys who help her make that decision.

Excruciating, excruciatingly. Courts most often encounter these terms when a writer is describing—often with a mixture of pride and dismay—a level of detail that was apparently (but probably not really) achieved only through intense physical or mental distress.

Exemplarily. Did you know that this is a word? Do you want your reader to stop and wonder the same thing?

Expansive, expansively. These terms often signal that the writer thinks (depending on which side she's on) that a definition or interpretation has gone too far—or just far enough.

Explosive, explosively. Like other terms rooted in weaponry and bloodshed, use these words sparingly to describe nonviolent situations.

Exponential, exponentially. These terms suggest a level of mathematical precision that may exceed the writer's intention to say only that something is increasing a lot and quickly.

Extraneous, extraneously. Using these terms offers a good way to give some extra space in your briefing to something irrelevant or unrelated to the issues.

Extreme, extremely. The law includes many instances in which "extremely" or "extreme" is a part of a legal standard, such as an "extremely dangerous condition" or "extremely offensive" physical contact. Whatever the wisdom of the use of these words in legislation or legal opinions codifying those standards, when left to their own devices, lawyers tend to add the adverb to adjectives in circumstances that just make it sound like the writer doth protest too much. Don't protest too much.

F.

Facial, facially, on its face. A word only lawyers could love outside the confines of a spa. Certain legal standards require you to use these terms, such as in "facial challenges" to statutes or jurisdiction. But those instances provide these words all the attention that they deserve.

Facilitative, facilitatively. These terms sound like a word that someone tried too hard to create. And they reward writers who use them by making them sound like they're trying too hard, too.

Fact-barren. I suppose this term sounds fancier than "fact-free" or "unsupported." Well, really just more showy, and not in a stylish way.

Failed, failing, failingly. Each of these terms gives a signal to courts that a premature declaration of victory is at hand. And, when coupled with "wholly," an exaggerated one at that.

Faintly. This word is hardly a study in precision to convey very slightly, or not a lot but more than not at all. But it's not a bad word if that's the best you can do.

Fake. This word is often used to broadly disparage something. But it has never meant "something I don't like."

Fallacious, fallaciously. If something is based on a mistaken belief or a logical fallacy, the court will get a lot more out of your explaining the shortcoming in the facts or reasoning than from your using either of these terms.

Fanciful, fancifully. This adjective features in some legal standards. Even in those contexts, it's a lot to have to say of someone or their ideas and allegations. There's no need to go—or sentence an opponent's arguments—to a realm of unreality if you don't have to.

Farcical, farcically. These terms offer a more theatrical way to call something ridiculous, but one that's no less inappropriate in legal briefing.

Fatal, fatally. It's become strangely commonplace to attach these terms to flaws, errors, and mistakes that, fortunately, pose no risk of death or even serious bodily injury.

Figurative, figuratively. These terms don't appear much in briefs or motions. But, when they do, it's a promising sign that the writer understands the literal meaning of "literally."

Finally. This adverb is most often used (and overused) to convey the writer's exasperation at how long it took for something to happen or get done. Where a long passage of time makes a difference to an argument or request for relief, using this word is a poor substitute for quantifying the length of time and letting your reader decide if it was excessive.

Fishing. This always seems to describe an "expedition." And together those two words form the most overused phrase in civil discovery practice.

Flagrant, flagrantly. Lawyers writing briefs or motions aren't referees. Let the judge make the call that something is so obviously or noticeably bad or offensive that the court can't ignore it. Your task is to stay in the game and make the case (sorry—sports metaphors only go so far) for that finding by laying out the facts and evidence.

Flatly. This word is handy when you want to leave no doubt that you are denying or refusing to do something.

Flippant, flippantly. Your opponent or someone in the history of a case may have made disrespectful remarks. You take that situation seriously by laying out the facts rather than describing them using these terms.

Foolish, foolishly. These terms only land well in legal briefing when directed to the writer herself with regret—and, even then, only when (your perhaps newfound) good judgment suggests that the self-deprecation is worth its cost.

Fortuitous, fortuitously. These are somewhat affected words to stand in for great phrases like "lucky chance" and "happy accident."

Frank, frankly. Courts are constrained to assume that the parties and counsel before them are being forthright and honest. Reading these terms often only raises concerns on that front about the writer using them.

Frustrated, frustratedly. If you're describing stymied efforts at something in a less fancy way than "stymied," this adjective may be fine. If you're describing your or your client's state of mind or emotional state, leave it out of your brief.

Frustrating, frustratingly. No matter how justified your annoyance may be, you'll sound like you're whining if you use these words.

Fully. The word of choice when you're assuring the court that you know or are willing and able to do something that you're maybe not so mindful of or eager to do. Such as (bracketed material left unspoken, of course) "if the Court needs us to put some meat on the bones [of this indefensible position], we are fully prepared to do so," or "counsel is fully aware of those contrary and binding authorities [that we've been ignoring]," or "fully cognizant of the court's prior warnings, defendant reurges its request [for that thing you implored us not to ask for again]."

Fulsome, fulsomely. These terms sound like they mean complete or fully filled, but, to many readers, they'll immediately bring to mind their other meaning: insincere and excessive. Which really isn't what you're going for if you're looking for a synonym for "abundant."

Fundamental, fundamentally. A fine way to describe something as involving basic elements or principles. A long-winded and unhelpful transitional adverb to tell the court, "What I'm about to say is important and true."

Funnily. Try saying this adverb out loud. It doesn't sound any better in your reader's head.

Futile, futilely. Courts have adopted a futility doctrine in several contexts. When you're not invoking those formal standards, you'll get better results by explaining how your opponent's argument or efforts are a sure loser or won't achieve anything useful.

G.

Galactic, galactically. Unless you're writing about the Milky Way, these words signal that something exaggerated or insulting is likely trailing behind.

Gamesmanship. Used in the sense of "playing games," this is a charge that's usually leveled by an attorney or party who is treating litigation like sport.

Garbled. This is another kind of fun word that sounds like its meaning. And it can be helpful when describing messages or communications that are confused, distorted, or jumbled.

Garden-variety. "Ordinary" or "common" work just as well, and without implicitly disparaging the quality of produce grown outside of commercial farms.

Gargantuan, gargantuanly, gigantic, gigantically, ginormous. The last one is probably not a real word. You can just say "really big" (if it really is gargantuan or gigantic). Or—probably better—"big." Or "large."

Generalized. It turns out that adding "-ize" to an unhelpfully unspecific term just signals to your reader that she'd better not hope for any precise details or concrete information to follow.

Glaring, glaringly. These terms only seem to show up to modify a "deficiency" or "fault." And what's most likely to stand out to a judge is the overstatement that will follow. Perhaps you can instead introduce the point with something like "what is missing is."

Glib, glibly. If someone's manner of writing or speech is a little too polished or smooth, you do yourself no favors by calling it out with these slick words and worrying your reader that everyone before her may be a bit slippery.

Gnarled. A word that sounds cool. If you're writing about an old tree.

Gnarly. Whatever utility this word may once have had, it was ruined by 1980s teenage slang. You might as well say "grody."

Good, goodly. One is a simple word that I could hardly advise you not to use in appropriate circumstances. The other will make you sound like a Victorian-era novelist who is desperate for an alternative after describing far too many large things.

Goofy, goofily. These words may fall on the mild side of the insult spectrum, but, unless you're working on a case about a silly You-Tube video or meme, there's got to be a better way to go.

Graceless, gracelessly. These terms offer a good descriptor of what a judge is likely to think of any effort to pin these words on your opponent.

Gracious, graciously. Unless you're sincerely describing someone's kindness or courtesy, you should avoid the nasty twist of commandeering these polite words into the service of incivility.

Grandiose, grandiosely. These terms are a bit too elaborate and potentially pretentious to employ for describing something or someone as being just that.

Granular, granularized, granularly. The devil may be in the details, but clarity and ease of reading favor "detailed" when you're describing analysis or reports that aren't high-level or broad. And the adverb form of "granular" sounds like the bits and pieces of the word should have remained separate.

Gratuitous, gratuitously. The American legal profession has adopted the all-purpose Latin phrase "pro bono" for describing services rendered free of charge. So these English terms are limited to describing something that someone did or said as being not necessary or not called for under the circumstances. Which description itself is usually unnecessary and uncalled for.

Grave, gravely. "Serious," "somber," or "worrying" can convey the same message without the overtones of death or dying.

Great, greatly. These terms are too often, and almost always unnecessarily, used to describe difficulties or something's importance. In popular retellings, Mark Twain is supposed to have added this modifier before "exaggerated" to make his famous (and reportedly misquoted) quip even funnier. As you hopefully already know, you're not Mark Twain—and he wasn't writing something serious for a judge.

Grisly. If death or murder are involved, and what happened matters, this adjective is no substitute for laying out the details. If death and murder aren't involved, this word shouldn't be in play.

Grizzled. This word almost always describes a veteran, apparently one with a lot of gray. This may feel more polite than just saying "old," but relying on this cliché is too high a price to pay for that small courtesy.

Groovy, groovily. No matter how eloquent, legal writing (and what it describes or discusses) will never make a reader feel this way. Save it for the next dance.

Groundbreaking, groundbreakingly. To convey that something reflects a new idea or approach, these words sound less jargony than "cutting-edge" and "leading-edge," less overblown than "radical" and "revolutionary," and less Old West than "pioneering" and "trailblazing." Of course, these words also bring to mind hard hats and golden shovels at the base of a future skyscraper.

Grudging, grudgingly. Does it really matter how excited your opponent was or wasn't to do what you'd been asking or what a judge ordered? Probably not. So spare your reader the extra ten letters and three syllables.

Gruesome, gruesomely. Think horror movie. If you find yourself with those kinds of facts, feel free to use these words. If you're not dealing with crimes or accidents involving injury or death, embellishing your writing with these terms may only distract your reader with thoughts of grisly details and slasher films.

H.

Hackneyed. This is a word that would probably describe itself if it weren't so antiquated and obscure. Better to describe a word or phrase as "overused"—even if this one isn't.

Halfhearted, halfheartedly. If someone's level of interest matters, these terms do sound better than "unenthusiastic" or "uninterested" (which may be confused with the legally significant and more positive "disinterested"). And the adverb form certainly rolls off the tongue in a way that "unenthusiastically" and "uninterestedly" never will.

Happy, happily. I'll confess that I've long been a fan of these words. Their wry, knowing understatement appeals to my sense of humor. But a rather smug take on coincidences and accidents and things that turn out all right despite themselves isn't to everyone's tastes. Tread lightly when you're not describing someone's cheerful disposition.

Hardly. When "almost never" or "almost not at all" feels too precise, this term rarely fails to make an appearance.

Hasty, hastily. These words read as a little less harsh than alternatives like "careless," "rash," or "impulsive." Just don't be too quick to comment on the speed or urgency with which someone else acted unless it really matters to what you're arguing to the court.

Helpful, helpfully. As with several other would-be compliments on these lists, in legal writing, these terms are often enlisted as sarcasm—sometimes delivering a chuckle but rarely offering much aid.

Highfalutin. This word may be cute, but it's too likely to draw roughly the same reaction as if you'd described something as "rootin tootin."

Highly. This word is pretty much always used to amplify a depiction of something as "relevant." But why freight your assertion with this intensifier unless it really matters whether something is very relevant or only somewhat relevant?

Historic, historical, historically. These are fine words to attach to descriptions of important past events. And they're great candidates to avoid to try to predict that the present case before you will one day be seen that way. Avoid the overstatement, and leave the assessments of legacies to future historians.

Honest, honestly. Most legal writers' use of these words follows an odd pattern. In my experience, forthright and sincere people worthy of trust unnecessarily qualify their statements with these terms, suggesting—falsely—that, without them, their readers would have good reason to doubt the truth of what they have to say. But folks who are stretching the facts and perhaps bending the truth tend not to use these words. Instead, they favor the hollow assurances "trust me" or "believe me." Which—justifiably—gives rise to the same suspicions.

Hopeful, hopefully. If the court might care that someone is full of optimism, by all means, use these words. But, if you wouldn't write "It is hoped" (and you shouldn't), you're not offering a judge anything more useful by starting your sentence with "Hopefully" instead.

Horrific, horrifically. You read these words, and "accident" or "injuries" are sure to follow. And, when that's so, there may be times when using these terms is a prudent exception to the "show, don't tell" rule.

Hot-blooded. Even if someone you're writing about has their dander up or is really angry, this word just doesn't carry the right connation for legal briefing.

Huge, hugely. Courts read more than you'd think about others' mistakes that are extremely large or enormous or, most often, "huge." What the degrees of mistakenness are, or how they matter for legal decisions, remain a mystery.

Humble, humbly. If you've got to say this on your own behalf, it probably isn't so.

Hyperbolic, hyperbolically. You might be correct to describe someone's statement this way. But do you really want to? For the same reason that we don't ever refer to your favorite school's costumed wildcat or mustang mascot as an anthropomorph.

Hypocritical, hypocritically. If someone's hypocrisy may matter to a judge, it's more powerful to present the facts and let it go unnamed—by you and probably (as you may have noticed) by the court as well.

I.

Idiotic, idiotically. It's not hard to see why, in a legal brief, you don't need to call someone an idiot or describe their actions as befitting an idiot, right?

Ignoble, ignobly. These are words that don't read any better than they sound. If you have a reason to be writing about someone's honor (or lack thereof), there must be a better option.

Ignominious, ignominiously. These terms almost always sound bad. After all, you've devoted five syllables to a fancy take-down. And why use these terms and blunt the impact of letting your reader know that someone's end, defeat, or retreat was disgraceful, shameful, or humiliating when—if it matters at all—you could just say that?

Ignorant, ignorantly. Words that, depending on the context, can show the writer's being generous—giving opposing counsel a pass because he was uninformed of a fact—or the opposite—using these terms more broadly to describe someone's character or qualities. Even if you don't intend to insult someone when pointing out their lack of knowledge or understanding, a judge is less likely to be put off by your telling her that someone was "unaware" of something that matters.

Ill-advised, ill-advisedly. These terms beg the question: According to whom? They can have something to add if the answer is a legal authority of some kind, a hindsight-assisted look at what already happened, or common sense. But, if the answer is only you, the writer, you'd be wise to avoid dropping this in as code for "this is not what I'd prefer."

Ill-informed, ill-informedly. These words play better than "stupid" and are less off-putting than "ignorant." But it feels like you might've started with "uninformed" and then decided to make your reader do just a little more work to take your point—and like you hate the sound of the English language if you choose to deploy the adverb.

Illegitimate, illegitimately. No one's mind isn't going straight to thoughts of parentage and wedlock with these words. Spare the thought of the hypothetical child, and go with one of the many other ways to describe something as unauthorized by law.

Illogical, illogically. If you're going to use these terms, you should be able to—but really shouldn't—describe the problem with an argument in formal logic terms.

Immediate, immediately. Some matters do require or warrant a court's attention, action, or ruling right now. For everything else, find another way to say "it's important to me."

Immense, immensely. The likelihood that you'll overstate your case with these words is huge. To avoid that enormous risk, maybe reserve their use for describing billionaires' wealth and the expanses of space and deserts.

Imminent, imminently. These terms describe the storm that'll arrive in a few minutes, not how qualified the Nobel laureate is to give a keynote address. And, in legal writing, courts see these terms either as part of a statement of facts involving death, disaster, or danger or as an exaggerated statement about procedural or deadline issues that only metaphorically involve those things.

Immutable, immutably. There's no avoiding that, with these terms, your reader is as likely to think that you're referring to someone who is not not capable of speech (an odd double negative, if ever there was one) as to something that cannot be changed.

Impenetrable, impenetrably. Some prose is, sadly, worthy of the comparison to a two-foot-thick titanium wall. Most isn't. Choose your targets wisely.

Impending. For a danger, disaster, storm, or crisis that's threatening on the horizon, there may be few better alternatives to these terms to convey the appropriate sense of doom and uncertainty. "Upcoming" sounds a bit scheduled, and "forthcoming" never made anyone's writing less clunky or stilted. Still, since calamity isn't usually really around the corner, better to rein in any nonessential catastrophizing.

Imperative, imperatively. These are words that'll be forever linked to Immanuel Kant and his theory of ethics known as "formalism." Avoid fussiness, and categorically exclude these terms based on the company they've kept.

Imperfect, imperfectly. Since most things in law and life are, using these terms is often superfluous unless you are also dealing with something truly faultless and need to point out the contrast.

Implacable, implacably. Hopefully you've no need to describe hatred or hostility this way. Otherwise, these words are a pretty overwrought way to tell a judge that your opponent won't—or at least hasn't—changed her mind.

Impossible, impossibly. Legal writers sometimes tell the court that some act or omission of an opponent has made something else "impossible." Like the boy who cried wolf, lawyers should claim impossibility only when something is in fact not possible, and not when it is only more difficult, burdensome, expensive, or time-consuming.

Impressive, impressively. Judges encounter these terms too often as vehicles for faint praise, withering irony, or a lead-in to a "but."

Impudent, impudently. I get it. You can't bring yourself to write "saucy," "sassy," or "cheeky"—and "insolent" sounds a bit too judgmental even for legal writing. But take the internal cue, ditch all these synonyms, and just describe the behavior in detail.

In all honesty. When witnesses are sworn in to tell the truth, the whole truth, and nothing but the truth, courts don't mean to suggest that that's optional for any other representation to a court. Why use a phrase that suggests you think it is and perhaps often take up that option?

Inaccurate, inaccurately. These terms are a pretty fair way to convey that something was miscalculated or based on a faulty understanding or a factual error. And a pretty weaselly way to say someone is lying.

Inadvertent, inadvertently. These are favored terms for excuses and responses to sanctions motions everywhere. Just don't confuse an accident or lack of attention with something you'd hoped no one would notice or see.

Inartful, inartfully. These words are reserved for running down another lawyer's performance. Outside a legal malpractice case, if you find these in your draft brief, it's probably time to omit the entire sentence.

Inauspicious, inauspiciously. Paired with "beginning" or "start," these terms can be good for a well-timed bit of snark once in a while. And the alternative "unpromising" sounds like it might not be a word. Just don't overdo it.

Incalculable, incalculably. There aren't a lot of things that modern computing and contemporary mathematics can't tally. Make sure that what you're describing with these terms is one of them.

Incessant, incessantly. To read these terms is to think of complaining and probably about bickering or quarreling or objecting. Draining, isn't it?

Inchoate, inchoately, incipient, incipiently. These terms may bring up memories—good or bad—of your first-year criminal law class. Whatever the state of your recollection, leave these terms in your memories, and, when you must, just say "not fully developed" or "not yet fully formed" or really anything else to get these ideas across.

Incidental, incidentally. One-word signals that what follows belongs in parentheses or a footnote—and, so, doesn't belong in your final draft at all.

Incoherent, incoherently. Although sometimes lost in a haze of conflict, there's a difference between being coherent and being correct. These terms should be reserved for arguments that you don't even know if you agree with because you genuinely can't understand and comprehend them.

Incompetent, incompetently. While useful and sometimes necessary in employment or criminal law contexts, you should be wary of leveling these charges at an attorney. The court will be.

Inconceivable, inconceivably. These terms describe something that is incapable of being imagined. There may be some outlandish rules (that are not rules) or concepts or notions that could fit that description and that a legal writer must address in a brief. But, in a rational world, it's unimaginable that there are many.

Inconclusive, inconclusively. Doctors and scientists may find themselves using these terms more frequently than lawyers do. But they do lend themselves to the kind of non-answer answer by which you're telling the court that you're not really telling it much—which is the way to go if that's all you've got, but not if it's not but it's all that you'd prefer to say.

Incongruent, incongruently. These words kind of make you think of geometry and angles or somesuch, don't they? Declaring something to be a "bad fit" or "mismatch" instead will spare your reader from any of that.

Inconsequential, inconsequentially. Fourteen-plus-letter words are a long way to travel to get to "it doesn't really matter."

Inconspicuous, inconspicuously. These words are showy ways to convey, depending on the circumstances, that something or someone is hidden, invisible, or unnoticeable.

Incontrovertible, incontrovertibly, indubitable, indubitably. It better really be. "Cannot be reasonably disputed" is more cumbersome but sometimes safer and more accurate.

Incorrect, incorrectly. Less severe than "wrong," less in-your-face than "mistaken," less technical sounding than "inaccurate," less lawyerly than "erroneous," less judgmental than "false" or "untrue." There's a lot to commend these terms—as long as you're actually saying that something doesn't line up with the facts and not just with your preferred outcome.

Incorrigible, incorrigibly. It's a harsh verdict to declare that something or someone can't possibly be corrected, improved, or reformed—one that you should hesitate to render unless you truly must.

Increasing, increasingly. When these show up in legal writing, you often get a sense that the writers' irritation and blood pressure levels could be described in the same way, in response to whatever it is that they're describing.

Indefinite, indefinitely. This adjective can be a vague way to convey that something is ambiguous or unclear or that it has no clear limits. As for the adverb, there's a difference that's sometimes lost in briefing between something that will go on for an unlimited period of time and something that just feels like it's going to go on forever.

Indescribable, indescribably. Lawyers are a verbally skilled bunch. There's not much that cannot be captured in words.

Indeterminate, indeterminately. These terms are a clunky way to convey one of several concepts that you could just lay out in basic terms. And the adverb reads like it was invented to stump players of the "say it ten times really fast" game.

Inept, ineptly. These terms amount to an insult that plays well in the precocious-preteen-flexing-their-expanding-vocabulary crowd but not in front of a judge.

Inevitable, inevitably. Don't confuse what you wanted to take place or hoped would happen with what was certain to occur or was unavoidable. The collapse of your opponent's legal strategy isn't equivalent to the fall of a boulder hanging off a cliff by a string.

Inexcusable, inexcusably. Litigation involves a lot of excusing, justifying, and pardoning. It's probably wise to let the court decide if someone or something is beyond the reach of those things.

Inexorable, inexorably. There's a lot more force in conveying through active verbs that something cannot be moved, stopped, or prevented—or even through a straightforward "unstoppable" or "unmovable" (no need to speak of the graceless "unpreventable")—than in relying on these fancy modifiers.

Infamous, infamously. Are you writing about an outlaw, gangster, war criminal, or serial killer? If not, take your villain as you find them, and save these terms for another day.

Infinite, infinitely. These terms come off as overstated or even mistaken when you use them (as legal writers often do) to mean a whole lot—since many readers naturally think of something boundless or immeasurable or limitless or, you know, infinity.

Inflated. This term seems to come before "view" any time a writer's opponent has a deficit in the self-awareness column.

Inherent, inherently. Courts encounter these terms enough with risks and dangers that it's rarely welcome to read lawyers' pitching these words to portray other matters as somehow essential or fundamental to the quality of something.

Inimical, inimically. These terms are truly hostile and unfriendly to clear, plain writing.

Innumerable, innumerably. These terms have concrete meanings, and there aren't many other words that convey them. But legal writers use these words to describe something that there's a lot of—but not, as the words' meanings demand, too many to be counted. Your opponent's arguments and the judge's rulings aren't, in fact, wrong in that many ways.

Inscrutable, inscrutably. These words offer a not-readily-understood way to describe something or someone as impossible or difficult to understand.

Insignificant, insignificantly. Perhaps it's a small step down the fancy word index, but it feels like a valuable one to move from these terms to "unimportant," "meaningless," and "small." And reaching for "not insignificant" is on a level with "not not saying" something.

Insipid, insipidly. These words sound a bit like the weak, bland, low-energy state that they convey. And that should be reason enough to avoid them.

Instant. Only lawyers describe the case at hand in the same way as on-the-go coffee or oatmeal. The word you're looking for is "this."

Insubstantial, insubstantially. These terms, which ought to be describing something as imaginary or lacking firmness, too often show up in legal briefs as long-winded ways to convey that an argument isn't persuasive or a factual position has little supporting evidence. These words are the stuff of ghosts or crumbling wafers, not disfavored theories.

Insulting. Telling the court that you have been disrespected and are offended—or that the judge has been and should be—rarely lands well on the page. Lay out the scenario for your reader, and let her decide how to react.

Intentional, intentionally. Intent is an important concept in the law. But, when ascribing intentionality to an opponent's actions or inaction, lawyers sometimes are engaged only in uncharitable speculation, which serves only to raise the temperature of the dispute. Unless intent is required for the relief that you're seeking, it's better to just describe the acts or omissions and let the court draw its own conclusions.

Interesting, interestingly. Using these words usually means that the writer finds something suspicious or probably false in some way—and hopes that the judge will, too.

Interminable, interminably. These terms don't even try to hide your annoyance. Points for candor, I suppose, but this kind of grumbling is rarely well received.

Intermittent, intermittently. You could describe something as happening "occasionally" or "periodically" or even "sporadically" and avoid calling to mind a way of dieting.

Intolerable, intolerably. Sometimes it adds something to an account of conditions or behavior to use these terms. But, more often, your reader will be more moved by actual descriptions of what someone cannot bear or endure.

Intractable, intractably. Using these terms instead of "difficult" or "stubborn" just adds one more problem (of comprehension) on top of whatever else you're laying on the court.

Irksome, irksomely. What a fun-sounding adjective. But it doesn't make it any more fun for a judge to read about how irritated or annoyed you are.

Ironic, ironically, irony. Legal writers, like others, often attribute irony to what is only contradictory or hypocritical or just bad or unfortunate. Other times they use the phrase "it is ironic that" to introduce a sentence in which they insult, ridicule, or mock an opponent. Don't use these words in formal legal writing—and don't try to use irony, properly understood.

Ironical. This is in dictionaries. It's a real word. But no one reading it will think that it is. It sounds more like a sad attempt to be "ironic" (air quotes intended) by mangling the term. Basically a mess. Just say "ironic," if you must.

Irresistible, irresistibly. Since most lawyers aren't physicists, these terms unavoidably and instantly bring to mind the romance-novel sense of the words rather than their foil-to-an-immovable-object meanings.

Irrespective, irrespectively. These terms make "regardless of" look crisp and pithy.

Irritating, irritatingly. It's hard to read these words and not conjure up images of sibling squabbles or awkward extended family get-togethers. Which presumably is not the vibe you're going for with the court.

It is important to note. This is an introductory phrase that suggests that other statements in your brief might be unimportant or unworthy of the court's full attention. Lose this verbiage, and give your reader confidence that you only include important facts or observations, all of which the reader should take note of.

It is no wonder, it is little wonder, is it any wonder. These are the rhetorical flourishes of choice for many writers attributing bad motives to an opponent without wanting to quite come out and say it directly. Avoid personal attacks and ascribing bad faith to opposing counsel or their clients unless you have no other choice. And, if you have no other choice, be direct and transparent about it.

J.

Judgmental, judgmentally. How often does any legal writing really need to describe how critical someone is? And this word choice is a bit fraught when directed to an institution that's in the business of handing down decisions and decrees.

Judgy. Is a court really the best audience for this way of describing someone as overly critical?

Jury-rigged. This is a nautical term for making do with what's at hand. But it's also an odd word to use in legal writing because it sounds like a reference to some conspiracy to corruptly influence a trial.

Just, justly. As an adjective (and accompanying adverb), these are nice, short words for the concept on which our system is based and depends. You really can't overuse them if you're taking these matters seriously. The same just can't be said of the four-letter adverb form.

K.

Keen, keenly. While it might matter if someone has above-average eyesight, when does it ever matter that someone is really, really aware of something? "Defendant knew about the binding precedent but was not keenly aware of it" hardly seems like much of an excuse.

Kind, kindly. Admirable qualities to be sure, but these words put you in mind of an English gentleman's overly polite request for you to stop doing something, don't they?

Knowing, knowingly. Save the glances and smiles for a rom-com screenplay. Otherwise, as with these terms' partners on the mens rea spectrum, judges get their fill in criminal, tort, and sanctions matters.

L.

Lamentable, lamentably, lamented, lamentedly. These words sound kind of poignant, right? Maybe even evocative? Perhaps. But one person's lament can be another's delight or joy, and it may be presumptuous to assume that the judge shares your disappointment or regret.

Large, largely. These are good, basic words that any reader will understand. As part of the project to combat wordiness and the overuse of big words (or, as the practice is more commonly known, sesquipedalianism), it's hard to fault writers for using these terms in moderation—bearing in mind that the adjective's meaning is hardly exact and that the adverb is at least weasel-word-adjacent.

Laudable, laudably, laudatory, laudatorily. These terms all express nice sentiments, but why make yourself or your reader worry about which one means expressing praise and which one means deserving it? Go with "praiseworthy" and "commendable" or, for that matter, "approving" or "complimentary."

Legitimate, legitimately. In everyday speech, these are often used in a loose sense to mean that something's acceptable or okay. But, because of their importance in legal contexts, legal writers should use these terms only in the more formal sense of conforming to governing laws or rules.

Liberal, liberally. This adjective has become so freighted with sociopolitical meaning. Avoid it unless you want some readers to be thinking of the week's Sunday morning shows.

Lightly. In legal writing, this word shows up to convey someone's indifference or lack of care or concern. But it's too easily slipped in with little force or weight, so use it sparingly.

Likely. You're probably overusing this word. A good rule of thumb: If you couldn't say that there is a high probability, give this term a pass.

Limited, limitedly. This adjective is another common word that doesn't give helpful information unless you explain how or by what. Otherwise, often accompanied by "very," it functions as a kind of weasel word. For its part, the adverb compels you to repeat it slowly a few times, like a spelling-bee competitor, as you struggle with whether it's a real word.

Limitless, limitlessly. In legal writing, these terms too often reflect a boundless capacity for exaggeration.

Loathsome, loathsomely. These words are a great way to describe a monster in a classic film. In legal briefing, take the high road, and reserve these terms for creepy-crawly, slimy creatures.

Loose, loosely. These words offer a useful signal that the legal writer is throwing off the restraints of precise reasoning or restrictions by rules and standards. A judge at least knows what to expect when told that the writer is "loosely speaking" or offering a "loose interpretation."

Loquacious, loquaciously. If meant as a compliment, these words and their intended messages are likely misguided. If used as an insult, you've approached irony but nothing else. (As an aside, was irony already dead for the coiners of these terms and their first, second, and third cousins "sesquipedalian," "polysyllabic," and "pellucid," or were they awash in too much of it?)

M.

Magical, magically. If, in a motion or a brief, you're describing something as "magical" or suggesting something happened "magically," you're probably not suggesting that your opponent (or, perhaps worse, the court) is a wizard. You're probably angry and ridiculing something. Calm down. Take a deep breath. And change your wording unless you really are talking about using spells or charms or a wand.

Manifest, manifestly. Courts have adopted these words, it seems, to make the meanings or application of certain terms of art and legal standards as unclear, obscure, or indistinct as possible. Legal writers' freelancing with their own ill-defined standards of "manifest unfairness" or "manifestly erroneous" does nothing to lift the fog.

Marginal, marginally. Lawyers seem to treat these terms as more exact than "slightly," perhaps because the implied reference to a margin conveys a sense that you're measuring against some concrete point of reference. But too often you're not.

Massive, massively. The words of choice when the amount of data is too much to manage (or search and produce in discovery) or some other effort is too immense for a court to require of you. And, if you read enough briefs, you'll be struck by the shocking number of really big failures that, reportedly, populate the litigation landscape.

Material, materially. These terms are closely related to "substantial" and "considerable" and just as difficult to define. Judges may know their meanings when they see them, but they don't need to see these terms outside the contexts of the many legal standards that require their use.

Meaningless, meaninglessly. There's a difference between points or arguments that you disagree with or dislike and statements that are empty or nothing more than gibberish. When you use these terms to target the former category, you render them, well, meaningless.

Measly. You risk yourself sounding small when, with an unavoidable tenor of contempt, you describe something as meager or slight using this angry word.

Miraculous, miraculously. If you're not genuinely referring to the supernatural or an act of God, take your tone down, and change your wording.

Momentous, momentously. Using these terms is usually a signal that what's being described is somewhat less than earth-shattering. They're best reserved for wedding toasts and describing the announcement of landmark Supreme Court decisions.

Most likely because. Lawyers sometimes must give a court their best guess or estimation as to some unknown event or thing. But, more often, "most likely because" signals that the writer is about to speculate about an opponent's motives or intentions—and to guess the very worst.

Mundane, mundanely. Neither the terms "dull" or "ordinary" nor what they fairly describe are made more interesting by using these fancier terms in their place.

Mysterious, mysteriously. Unless you're writing about something fit for a detective novel or television news magazine, when your reader sees these terms, she knows that sarcasm or innuendo are sure to follow.

N.

Naive, naively. Legal writers occasionally explain witnesses' testimony or belittle opponents' conduct with these terms. More often these words are deployed to excuse the writers' own innocent or gullible reliance on an opponent's treachery. But the babe-in-the-woods routine can be a hard sell—and isn't often required for the point that the writer needs to make.

Narrow, narrowly. These words sometimes offer an apt and important way to describe a law's interpretation—although not every construction that doesn't support a party's preferred outcome fits this bill. And these terms are, unfortunately, less often used as a worthy vehicle to describe an escape—ideally as part of an engaging factual story.

Nearly. Judges need to be told that something was "almost but not quite" not nearly as often as lawyers seem to think. Put more meat on the bones when you can, and, if you can't, stand ready to discard this squishy modifier.

Negligible, negligibly. These are more elaborate words than you'd think you'd need to describe something as unworthy of even considering.

Never-ending, never-endingly. These terms usually reflect a fitting account of how the entire case feels to a judge by the time he is reading one side or the other describe something this way.

Noble, nobly. These words are probably not being used as a tribute to someone. They may appear, at best, as a backhanded compliment or, more likely, sarcasm: "New counsel finally offered to present his client for deposition—a noble gesture after the course of negotiations in the months before." Unless you're discussing someone with a feudal title, probably best to leave these words alone.

Noisy, noisily. This adjective is a simple word for a simple concept. But, while the adverb may not be loud, it just sounds bad.

Nonessential, nonessentially. These words are fine examples of bureaucratic language (or officialese or bureaucratese) that likely did not exist—or need to—before we had a robust administrative state.

Nonexistent. So few things (that we know of) actually are. It's a testament to lawyers' collective imaginations—and chutzpah—that they can so often use this term to exaggerate even a lack of existence.

Nonplussed. This is a word that sounds good but doesn't work with modern audiences, who'll hear it to mean that someone isn't bothered or surprised by something. But, formally at least, it describes someone as being perplexed. In short, it's a word with a surprisingly confusing meaning that risks leaving your reader experiencing what it's properly meant to describe.

Nonsensical, nonsensically. This isn't how you describe a losing argument or weak reasoning; it's how you describe logical or analytical gibberish. If what you're describing has more meaning and makes more sense than a baby's babble, go another route.

Notable, notably, noteworthy, noteworthily. These terms function as a kind of single-word throat-clearer, a more succinct way of saying "it may be noted that" or "it should be remembered that." And "noteworthily" proves that you can stick "-ly" on the end of just about any adjective and come up with an adverb—which does little to recommend this one or adverbs more generally.

Nullified, nullifying. These are words with exclusively legal meanings. No matter how cool they may sound, reserve them for their proper contexts, when no other, less lawyerly term will do.

Numerous. Much of the time, or perhaps more than some, you may not be able to be more specific than using this term. For every other occasion, there are actual numbers.

O.

Obedient, obediently. If you're not writing about a well-trained canine companion, you may as well be in your reader's subconscious. But your opponent isn't a dog. Probably.

Obeisant, obeisantly. These terms are useful for distracting a judge from the courtesy or respect that you're intending to write about by appearing to badly misspell "obedient."

Obfuscated, obfuscating. These terms sound fun. I suppose it's the *b* followed by the *f*. But, if you mean to convey that someone is trying to make something unclear or harder to understand, you don't need to use a word that provides an example of doing just that.

Oblique, obliquely. These terms offer a pretty obscure way to say that something isn't straightforward. Rich in irony, perhaps, but not so much in clarity.

Obliterated. Go ahead and remove this word completely from your repertoire unless you're writing about a serial number on a stolen firearm.

Obnoxious, obnoxiously. Fairly or not, dropping this descriptor on something can itself be seen as annoying. Just objectively describe the behavior or statements, and let the reader attach this label herself.

Obscene, obscenely. Unless you're using the legal term of art, your readers likely know that they'd prefer not to see any other uses of these terms.

Obsequious, obsequiously. These terms are useful when equating someone to a well-trained animal isn't insulting enough. If you wouldn't write "bootlicking" or "toadyish" in your brief, give these words a miss as well.

Obsolescent, obsolescently. These are fancy words for reaching a point that's described by another fancy word. These terms may not themselves be obsolete in every context, but, for the sake of your reader, don't double down—just say "becoming obsolete."

Obsolete, obsoletely. The adverb form feels like it exists only to be used to dare someone to try to use it in speech. But the adjective is admittedly hard to replace—"outdated" or "out of date" might work, perhaps, but they don't really capture the idea of no longer being in use or needed. And most readers won't trip over "obsolete." Just be sure to deploy it only for words or laws or technology that really are out of circulation.

Obstinate, obstinately. Some legal standards for sanctioning parties or lawyers use these words. And that should tell you all you need to know about how inflammatory their use outside of that context is likely to be.

Obtrusive, obtrusively. If you stick one of these words in a sentence in a brief, it'll likely be prominent or noticeable to your reader—but not as a welcome sight, as she grabs a dictionary (or searches online) to find its meaning. And then learns it means just that.

Obtuse, obtusely. This is a really hoity-toity insult that'll make any opponent who knows what it means mad if you direct it at them. For the rest of your readers, they'll likely be forced to cycle through "obscure," "obtuse," and "abstruse" in their mind—and, likely, a dictionary—to sort out what you mean.

Obviated, obviating. I have used the verb form of these words too many times myself. Remove the need for your reader to check their meanings, and just employ a variation of "avoid," "prevent," or "make unnecessary."

Off-putting. This is kind of a fun-sounding word, and one that most readers will understand. But you don't need to be putting your own reaction to, or feelings about, something into your legal writing.

Omnifarious. As in wicked meditation. Or maybe it's meditative wickedness? (Sound it out—with a long *o*.) Actually, it means something takes all kinds of varieties or forms. Now take a deep breath, and let this word go.

Onerous, onerously. A sure sign that, on the reality-check scale, the magnitude of the burden that the writer is describing with these terms falls somewhere below where the writer is claiming.

Ostentatious, ostentatiously. Be wary of using words that provide pretty great examples of the meanings they intend to convey.

Outraged, outrageous, outrageously. Maybe judges are less easily shocked or offended than many people, but these terms seem to show up an awful lot to describe the merely undesirable, unwelcome, or unwished-for.

Overblown. This is how legal writers describe their opponents' or a court's concerns when the writer really is worried that they may have a point.

Overheated, overheatedly. These words are almost always followed by "rhetoric"—and likely as part of a prime example of that very phenomenon.

Overly. While perhaps prone to overuse, this term is at least more compact than its close cousin "excessively."

Overrated. Throwing this word at a concept or opponent likely won't do anything for your reader other than distract her with thoughts of a mocking stadium chant.

Overt, overtly. Sometimes it's readily apparent that something is open and in plain sight—and, when it is, your reader doesn't need you to state the obvious.

Oxymoronic, oxymoronically. It's difficult to imagine why you'd need to discuss with a court whether a combination of words looks contradictory but isn't. And the adverbial form looks and sounds like it should be the last word in any debate over whether adverbs are awful.

P.

Paradigmatic, paradigmatically. These terms are perhaps the quintessential example of a fancy word for a straightforward concept. They're a model of wordiness to enable you to bypass such disyllabic pretenders as "classic" or "standard."

Paradoxical, paradoxically. Like irony, legal writers actually need to call out this concept even less often than they manage to do so correctly. If the context doesn't warrant devoting a sentence to saying "this is a paradox," it doesn't merit using these verbal mouthfuls either.

Parenthetical, parenthetically. Thanks to decades of case citations, lawyers have turned an adjective into a noun. You probably can't avoid either one if you must write about citations. But you can dodge the adverb and either use something like "by the way" or, better yet, decide against including any announced digression or aside in your brief.

Partial, partially. These terms almost never appear in the sense of "biased." Instead, these terms denote the great middle gray area of "some but not all" in which so many arguments and rulings reside—and these words do so helpfully if the writer goes on to explain the metes and bounds of what's in play.

Partly. This is a somewhat but not completely useless word.

Patently. This adverb almost always precedes "obvious." What distinguishes something obvious from the patently obvious is a bit of a mystery but not one worth solving. Better just to leave this word to intellectual property lawyers to use in its noun form.

Pathetic, pathetically. These words may once have described someone or something as deserving of pity, compassion, or sympathy. But now those feelings are nowhere to be found when judges encounter these insults in a motion or a brief.

Patronizing, patronizingly. No one should tolerate bullying or harassment in law practice. But, short of that level of misconduct, using these terms to call out someone's behavior that disingenuously appears helpful or kind while reflecting a superior attitude usually falls flat and leads to unproductive finger-pointing. It's better to take statements at face value, express gratitude to the would-be helper for the advice, and stick to the points that you need to make about what really matters to the court.

Peculiar, peculiarly. An especially fancy way to call something odd or strange or to say "that's so her." Which ought to be quite unusual in legal writing.

Pedantic, pedantically. Maybe I shouldn't touch these words in a book like this. *See* "Curmudgeonly."

Pejorative, pejoratively. If you find yourself reaching for one of these terms while writing a brief, it's a good time to note that, when lawyers are disparaging or belittling their opponents' arguments or rhetoric as disparaging or belittling, things are likely going south in the case overall.

Pellucid, pellucidly. These terms offer a hard-to-understand way to describe something as easy to understand. And they seem to be a magnet for passive voice, to boot—think "make pellucid." And no one really talks this way.

Penultimate, penultimately. This is a really fancy word for next-to-last. And it just gets fancier (and not in a good way) when adding "-ly" to make it an adverb.

Perennial, perennially. There's a real chance your reader is thinking about planting his garden next spring when he reads one of these terms.

Perfectly. This word is helpful for describing someone performing in a way that could not have been done better. Otherwise, this term offers a signal either that the writer is irritated at her opponent's position that the opponent (apparently) knows all too well is wrong or that the writer is making what is a very, very reasonable request. Which, to be perfectly frank, is neither helpful nor welcome.

Perfunctory, perfunctorily. These are big words often tossed out, without much care or concern for a writing's ease of reading, to convey a lack of interest or reflection.

Perplexed, perplexedly, perplexing, perplexingly. Like their *x*-bearing counterpart "flummox," these words sound great and sound like what they mean. But you'd better be confident that the judge will find the object or source of your confusion just as befuddling as you do—or else she may just be mystified at your professed lack of understanding.

Perpetual, perpetually. These terms almost always involve an overstatement in legal writing since most events and human behavior don't actually outlast a pendulum clock (which, I know, is not actually a perpetual motion machine).

Persistent, persistently. There's often a tone of contempt and disapproval with these terms, no matter how neutral the context.

Philistine. Admittedly, very few judges have probably ever run across this adjective in a brief. But it wouldn't fairly mark them as uncultured if their first reaction on reading it was to wonder which Greek city-state you're referring to and why you'd be doing so in the first place.

Pigheaded, pigheadedly. You're tempted to want to read a brief or motion that has descended to this level of discourse, right? To appreciate it as self-parody or a cautionary tale. But you don't want your name on it.

Pleasant, pleasantly. In legal briefing, these words often importantly convey a special way of being surprised.

Plethora. Ick. This is a fifty-cent word best left behind in high school. Sounds like a kid trying out his SAT vocabulary words. Or, if we're being really frank, some kind of tropical reptile or disease. Choose another word. There are many (there's one!) to choose from.

Poached. You can't really expect the judge not to think about breakfast when you use this word.

Pointless, pointlessly. These terms are often used to describe an exercise or discussion that probably needs to happen but that the writer wishes would end or just go away.

Possible, possibly, potential, potentially. At their worst, these terms call to mind the always helpful witness answer that "anything's possible." These terms are unavoidable at times, but your writing should at least rise above the spirit of that kind of overused response.

Post hoc. Unlike its Latin relative "ad hoc," there is a better way to describe something as being offered only after the fact. And, when "after-the-fact" won't do, you can grapple with whether "revisionary" or "retroactive" are needed. Or you could just use basic English words to explain why the judge shouldn't accept your opponent's explanation or justification.

Precious, preciously. Lawyers probably aren't writing about jewels, family heirlooms, or porcelain miniatures when they use these terms in a brief. If you are, good on you. If not, using these words to describe something as excessively refined is too often excessively refined.

Precipitous, precipitously. There's no need to distract your reader with visions of cliffs and slopes when "steep," "sudden," "sharp," and even "abrupt" are ready to roll.

Precise, precisely. These terms offer the lesser of two evils (well, modifiers or, more specifically, amplifiers) if they prevent a legal writer from using a bold or italicized "is." But, still, your reader can be trusted to understand that you're confirming or agreeing with something without the need for any extra nudge.

Predictable, predictably. Lawyers often add an extra dash of negativity to these terms to describe an opponent as behaving in a way that was expected—and to be lamented or scorned.

Preeminent, preeminently. What every lawyer says about her expert witnesses and their qualifications. No matter what.

Prefatory, prefatorily. Calling something a "preface" instead of an "introduction" is already a bit much. But turning the noun into an adjective and adverb—because "introductory," "opening," or "beginning" would just be too easy on your reader—is excessive.

Preposterous, preposterously. It should be a rare occasion that you're calling something out as silly or ridiculously unreasonable. And, so, if and when you do, you really shouldn't need to go beyond "absurd" and turn to these cumbersome terms to mix things up.

Presumable, presumably. When used in connection with events or historical facts, this adverb conveys that a lawyer is describing what she really thinks happened or why, even though she can't be certain. When used in connection with an opponent's argument or litigation positions, the adverb gives away that the lawyer is pretty certain that what's she about to describe is not her opponent's true intention or motivation. For civility's sake, stick to the first context for this overused term.

Presumptive, presumptively, presumptuous, presumptuously. Presumptions play an important role with several burdens of production and persuasion. "Presumptive" can be a handy shorthand—and doesn't carry an air of disdain or disapproval—in those contexts. But, when used in place of "presumptuous" to convey that your opponent or the court is making an unwarranted inference or assumption, you're better off saying that straight out and explaining why. Using these words in that context just adds a negative flavor that won't change the mind or ways of the would-be object of your condemnation and won't itself persuade any judge looking for facts to try to assess whether you're right.

Prime. This word is likely not being used to describe a number that cannot be divided evenly into another number. And it's too often misused to introduce an example that is not perfect or even typical of other instances of the subject at hand.

Primitive, primitively. This is a great word to describe something from an early era of history. And it's an unnecessarily insulting way to tell a judge that you believe someone or something is old-fashioned, simple, unsophisticated, crude, or unrefined.

Prior to. Using two words is almost never better than using just one. And "before" is a good one. Let it do its work.

Probative, probatively. Using these terms usually just proves that you know how to sound like a lawyer.

Problematic, problematically. Whatever else may be said about it, the law provides rules and standards. Apply those, and avoid these undefined charges.

Profane, profanely. This is a good adjective to refer to someone using profanity. And it's a highfalutin word to describe something as vulgar.

Profanity. Just don't. Not even in Latin. Unless you're quoting something said or written in connection with essential facts of the case.

Profound, profoundly. These terms offer all the undefined scope of "extremely" or "greatly" but with the addition of a faint hint of trying to sound deep or intellectual.

Prolix, prolixly. These are short but fancy words to describe using too many (and often fancy) words. "Wordy" will do just fine.

But avoid the adverbs: "Wordily," like "prolixly," sounds like you're pulling a prank on the English language.

Prompt, promptly. In legal writing, these terms mean at the deadline, but not after—and somehow they never involve filing something early.

Proper, properly. These words are a bit ambiguous (do you mean accurate or just okay?), a bit British, and more than a bit overused when more precise terms for either meaning are available.

Prophetic, prophetical, prophetically. Lawyers and judges can certainly be wise, but don't go overboard with comparisons to seers and fortunetellers.

Prophylactic, prophylactically. However much writers might want these terms to involve a broader context, you just can't escape the health-related connotations.

Propitious, propitiously. These fancy words don't even sound favorable or auspicious. They kind of sound like a diagnosis that you don't want.

Proverbial, proverbially. In practice, these terms act as unnecessary highlighting to alert your reader that they're about to encounter a saying that's already well-known to them (and most others). While proverbs and idioms themselves can enhance your writing, they lose a bit in the telling when pointed out or announced like this.

Provocative, provocatively. Like it or not, the more R-rated connotations of these terms will be hard for many readers to ignore.

Purported, purportedly. These words are sometimes misused to refer to something that someone tries or attempts (improperly or unsuccessfully) rather than something that someone only claims or alleges. And, in any sense, they're too often used to do nothing but cast shade.

Purposeful, purposefully, purposely. These terms read as if they're being coined in mid-speech—as if you've realized that there must be an adjective for acting with an aim or objective (or at least not by accident) and you're piecing it together in real time.

Pursuant to. It's so tempting to use this unwieldy phrase. But just let it go, and use "under." It really does read and sound better.

Putrid, putridly. These are kind of awesome words because they sound like their subjects smell. But one shudders to imagine their use in legal writing outside of a statement of facts involving rotten food.

Q.

Quaint, quaintly. These are a funny kind of compliment that plays much better when speaking than writing, where it's likely to hit your reader as more odd or peculiar than pleasant or charming.

Qualified, qualifiedly. Save these for the many legal terms of art that include them, or for discussing an employment law plaintiff's skills or credentials. The law presents enough challenges with defining the parameters of several "qualified" standards as it is.

Quality. This isn't commonly used in legal writing as an adjective, but it's well known to English football fans. Leave it for the British tabloids' coverage of your club's best goals or transfer targets.

Questionable, questionably. One thing that's not open to question: using these squishy terms won't add any force to your arguments or clarity to your reasoning.

Quintessential, quintessentially. If you're truly addressing a perfect example of something, perhaps you've earned the right to deploy these pretty-close-to-perfect examples of unnecessarily fancy words. Or you could just spend your fourteen letters on "perfect example" and pick up some clarity to boot.

Quixotic, quixotically. There's an element of someone's being admirably idealistic that too often gets lost in legal writers' use of these terms as a way to knock the merely impractical, hopeless, or misguided. Regardless, save the lyricism and romanticism for another context.

Quotidian. This word means "daily." Seriously. No one wants to decipher what you mean by an injured plaintiff's missing out on the "quotidian pleasures of childhood." Just say "daily." Or "everyday."

R.

Radical, radically. It's hard not to think of activists when seeing these words. And, as they're often used, they are redundant and only beg the question of what exactly would count as modestly transforming something through a moderate overhaul.

Random, randomly. These terms are the words of choice to describe something chosen or determined by chance. But using them—as legal writers sometimes do—to describe something that seems or feels odd or weird to the reader still, in formal writing, feels odd and weird.

Rare, rarely. Legal writers infrequently use this adjective in the sense of a compliment. And otherwise, unless these words are used to describe something that appears no more frequently than a bird of a species approaching extinction, lawyers are usually overusing these terms.

Reasonable, reasonably. Fundamental standards in tort and criminal law, among others, depend on these terms. Judges interact with the hypothetical "reasonable person" all the time. Enough so that, outside the contexts of these standards and doctrines, complaints about an opponent's "not being reasonable" are as unwelcome as they are frequent. Show the court the care, sensibility, and judgment that you feel you're not getting, and take the time to explain what your opponent is or isn't doing that he shouldn't or should be.

Regrettable, regrettably. Using these words is not a bad way to start off a letter to kids' parents announcing that you cancelled the field trip due to a chicken pox outbreak—if you're a grade school principal. But, in a submission to a court, these terms usually signal an explanation that'll replace the accountability piece with the worst kind of passive voice, where mistakes were made and deadlines couldn't be met. Use them sparingly.

Relative, relatively. These are somewhat helpful words when the basis for comparison is clear. They're absolutely weaselly words when it's not.

Reluctant, reluctantly. When attacking an opponent or seeking sanctions, lawyers often use these terms to tell judges how disinclined or loath the writer is to be doing what he's doing. Perhaps it's understandable that the court may be hesitant to believe it every time.

Remote, remotely. If you use these terms, there's only a slight possibility that your reader won't first be thinking of televisions and teleworking. Sometimes events and trends in life overtake original meanings.

Repeated, repeatedly. These terms often show up as a kind of drum that attorneys bang over and over in frustration after having already explained to the court what their opponent has been or has not been doing.

Repentant, repentantly. Courts mostly read about how an opponent should be confessing and making amends but isn't, and they rarely see these terms directed to the writer or his client. Repentance for thee but not for me, I guess.

Repetitive, repetitively. These are useful terms so long as you're comfortable conveying—depending on the context—annoyance or boredom.

Repudiated, repudiating. These are fine, lawyerly words to deploy when you want to reject the challenge to write the way that people talk (when they speak well).

Repugnant, repugnantly. Hopefully you never encounter anything so disgusting or objectionable as to merit using these terms. And, no, conflicts or incompatibility between laws or rules never merits writing "repugnant to"—which, while perhaps not disgusting, may at the least offend your reader's sensibilities.

Resounding, resoundingly. These are the verbal vehicles of choice when it's not enough to just declare victory or relish another's defeat and only spiking the football will do.

Respect, respectful, respectfully. These terms are often used in phrases such as "with all due respect," "meaning no disrespect," and "without intending any disrespect." But you will either show respect in what you say and how you say it, or you won't. Incanting these empty phrases has no effect on your being respectful (or not). Beginning a disrespectful discussion with "meaning no disrespect" only shows how hollow that phrase is. And "with all due respect" is always an empty vessel because it begs the question how much respect is "due"—which often, in light of what follows this phrase, apparently is quite little. And telling the court that you "respectfully request" some relief implies that you might have some less-than-respectful requests that you're holding back.

Retaliatory, retaliatorily. Several causes of actions or legal standards involve this adjective. But using the adverb feels like you're taking revenge on your reader for some reason.

Rhetorical questions. Have you ever seen a rhetorical question used effectively? Have you? Well, of course you have. It's not a useless device. But what were you doing in the seconds after reading that question? You were probably trying to prove me wrong. Because that's what a rhetorical question does—it challenges the audience to come up with an answer other than the one that the speaker is implying must be the only option. You don't want to be in that posture with a judge. Your goal should be to have the reader going along with you at every step. Putting a challenge to the court—inviting the judge to come up with why your question doesn't require the answer that you are assuming that it does—doesn't advance that goal.

Ridiculous, ridiculously. Courts aren't in the business of mocking or laughing at parties, lawyers, or arguments. Don't invite them to do so.

Rough, roughly. These words are useful when even "approximate" is too exact. Sometimes that's the best you can do, but not too often.

Routine, routinely. Legal writers use these terms to describe how courts hold things: "This court has routinely held that X." But too often that's an exaggeration—and the writer has confused the favorable or wished-for with the common or frequent. Unless something really is a matter of routine—applying the basic Federal Rule of Civil Procedure 56 standards to summary judgment motions, for example—and the fact that it is routine matters for some reason, avoid the temptation to run the risk of (often unnecessarily) overstating the strength of your favorable authority.

Rude, rudely. Describing something or someone as "rude" to a reader who wasn't present to observe the behavior or comments is hardly ever effective. What is or is not rude so often depends on the eye of the beholder that the writer does better to repeat the exact statements or actions without commentary and let the reader decide if they cross the rudeness line—to whatever extent that even matters under any legal standard.

S.

Sacred, sacredly, sacrosanct. These terms show up in the secular sense of being of high value or not open to question or attack. But bear in mind that it's hard to fully separate the religious connotations from any use of these words.

Sadly. Like its opposite "happily," I can't quite quit this word in casual conversation. But, regrettably, it's usually deployed with a bit too much snark for most audiences that you're writing for.

Sagacious, sagaciously, sage, sagely. These are nice compliments if you or your advice can get them. But prudence dictates sticking with the simpler and more familiar "wise" or "discerning" or even some variation of "has good judgment."

Salient, saliently. Legal writers use these terms to sound lawyerly or distract their audience when describing a point that's the most important or noticeable. Offer your reader the path of least resistance by using easier and simpler terms and letting your actual, important point be the star of the show.

Sanctimonious, sanctimoniously. It's hard to imagine when you'd need to describe someone as hypocritically pious or pretentiously morally superior. Or why you'd want to do so using these terms that sound like they may open you up to the classic "I'm rubber, you're glue" defense.

Sanguine, sanguinely. These words sound like they'd mean some kind of groovy calm. It'd be cool if they did. But instead they offer a great way to confuse and misdirect your audience from focusing on your hopeful or optimistic report.

Saucy, saucily. These words not only might describe a pirate but sound like something one might say. And the adverb sounds like an island in the Mediterranean Sea.

Scarce, scarcely. The adverb often shows up in the midst of "there could…have been"—which is hardly any Plain English instructor's dream sentence structure. Together, these versatile terms can bring an archaic tone to your writing, if that's what you're going for.

Seldom. This is the rare example of an adverb that shouldn't take the "-ly." But, even if "seldomly" isn't a real word, the proper dual-purpose adjective-adverb gives writing an antique quality that has little to commend it for all but infrequent use.

Self-evident, self-evidently. Some truths are. For all the others, avoid an "oh, well, if you say so" reaction, and make the effort to show your work with proof and reasoning.

Self-explanatory, self-explanatorily. These terms offer a polite code to signal that you have no persuasive or coherent description of or justification for something. Go ahead and explain it as best you can—your reader won't mind.

Self-serving. In litigation, it's often surprising to read this term levied as a criticism of testimony or affidavits. It suggests that the writer may misapprehend the goal of the overall enterprise. There's a time and place for charity, altruism, and generosity, but it's generally not on the witness stand or in a summary judgment response when a party is trying to win a case.

Selfish, selfishly. This feels a bit personal, doesn't it? If you're referring to something you want ("we'd selfishly prefer"), you're inserting yourself too much as the writer. If you're referring to an opponent, it might be true, but saying it isn't likely to be productive.

Semantic, semantically. Assuming that your reader fully appreciates their meanings, these terms always involve a bit too much verbal navel-gazing to be of aid to crisp, clear writing.

Senseless, senselessly. These words seem to always attach to "violence" or "violent," and in a well-intentioned way. But, in most contexts in which you'd use these terms, is there another kind?

Sensible, sensibly. These words often come off as something of a backhanded compliment ("that seems sensible") when not describing shoes in the manner of a 1950s schoolchild. You can usually do better.

Severe, severely. Legal writers often turn to these terms as more eloquent alternatives to "a whole lot" and "in a big way." But it's always worth asking yourself what, if anything, a judge gets from reading that an opponent didn't only underestimate something but rather "severely underestimated" it. You may be overestimating the added value.

Shaky, shakily. This is the adjective of choice when describing an opponent's evidence—on those occasions when a lawyer acknowledges that they have any. And the adverb sounds like it's likely to fall apart the moment you say it.

Shameless, shamelessly. This tells your reader that someone is not only acting wrongly, foolishly, or disgracefully but that he has no capacity to recognize or care about it. If ever the "show, don't tell" advice had some teeth, it's in advising you not to deliver this strong medicine.

Sharp, sharply. These terms appear when writers want to let a judge know that they don't just disagree with something but also that they're angry. Which is fine, I suppose, if that's your point for some reason.

Shining. This word is often attached to "example" to point a spotlight on it, but it's too often darkened with more than a little sarcasm.

Shocking, shockingly. Maybe it's not true that nothing is shocking, but—while courts hear about criminal conduct that truly is, and while some legal standards require one's conscience to be shocked—far less is shocking than many briefs would have you believe.

Short, shortly. A reliable indication that you'll be waiting a while longer.

Shortsighted, shortsightedly. Before you accuse an opponent of lacking foresight or imagination, step into the shoes that they were wearing at the decision's time and consider what they knew or thought then. Hindsight bias is a real thing.

Shrewd, shrewdly. These words sure don't sound like compliments, do they? As a general rule, give a miss to "mousy," "ratty," "squirrely," "weaselly," and any other adjectives based on moles, rodents, or the like.

Sickening, sickeningly. Legal writers more often intend the disgust-inducing sense than the sickness- or nausea-inducing sense of these terms. But the words themselves suggest a physical response that, because it's likely missing from a reasonable reaction to some position that you really don't like, provides good cause to turn elsewhere.

Significant, significantly. About half the time a judge reads these terms, she knows she's hearing about something that's unimportant or that she didn't need to notice.

Simple, simplified, simplifying, simplistic. These terms come off alright when the writer is objectively describing something without judgment. But using them to belittle ideas or efforts can backfire if your reader instead sees clarity, elegance, or even sophistication.

Singular, singularly. As with other absolute or unqualified descriptors, you'll do your writing more harm than good when using these terms if what you're describing doesn't really stand out from a crowd.

Skeptical, skeptically. That you are, and believe the judge should be, doubtful about an opponent's positions or arguments may be one of the least surprising (or helpful) things that the judge reads that day.

Slavish, slavishly. Words that combine "-ish" and a reference to human bondage to mean something less grave than forced servitude might never have been a good idea. They certainly don't play well in this century.

Slight, slightly. No one expects lawyers to describe everything with exact percentages or precise measurements. But, if there's even the smallest possibility to do so instead of reaching for these terms, you should.

Sloppy, sloppily. Calling up for the court images of young kids' rooms, school cafeteria meals, and drunks is probably more (or maybe less) than you intend to do when using these words to dunk on someone's work or thinking. Keep your rhetoric a bit cleaner than this.

Smooth, smoothly. Legal writers use these words more often to explain how things didn't go—because litigation and briefs don't traffic much in matters that present no difficulties or problems.

Solemn, solemnly. Leave these terms to the oaths and vows that lawyers and witnesses must take and judges administer.

Sparing, sparingly. The adjective sounds terribly old-fashioned, particularly when coupled with "of" or "with."

Speaks for itself. This is a phrase long favored by lawyers that, in briefs, often comes just before the writer—instead of quoting the supposedly self-explanatory text—launches into a long discussion that suggests perhaps the thing doesn't speak so clearly on its own behalf.

Spectacular, spectacularly. These terms call to mind fireworks displays and mountain ranges. Probably best to find another word if you don't want your reader thinking fondly of the Fourth of July in Colorado.

Sporting, sportingly. Unless you're writing about the adventures of English aristocrats at a country estate, these words most likely show up associated somehow with "chance," which is kind of a more fun but indirect way to describe roughly the same odds as a preponderance.

Square, squarely. These terms function like unnecessary underlining when describing how things fall on someone's shoulders, someone must face an issue, or something is in the middle.

Stern, sternly. These words describe a kind of warning that is different from, it seems, the oh-so-common gentle or easygoing admonishment.

Sticky, stickily. This adjective is a fun way to describe something as difficult, but it's perhaps a little too suggestive of bubble gum for some readers. And the adverb reads and sounds like it was constructed by someone who hates the English language.

Straightforward, straightforwardly. These are direct and easy-to-understand terms, which, regrettably, require sticking together two longish direct and simple words to create a string of letters that's more than half the length of the alphabet.

Strange, strangely. These terms play better in conversation or speeches than in legal writing—probably because they only come off well when directed at the speaker and not someone else.

Strict, strictly. These words play outsized roles in many legal terms of art and cannot be avoided. But judges can do without "strictly speaking"—which, like "in point of fact" or "in actual fact," is at best unnecessary to tell a court that you're telling it something straight up or, at worst, suggests the judge should take a closer look at any statements that you don't warrant with these phrases.

Strike at the very core of. This phrase is usually followed by "our judicial system" or "judicial process." Some things do threaten or strike at the justice system's core. But they rarely are the subject of a brief using this hackneyed phrase.

Strong, strongly. In legal writing, these are the stuff not of muscles but of "disagreements" and "chances" and, sometimes, "cases." And, too often, these terms couldn't fairly describe the clarity and effectiveness of any legal writing using these nebulous words.

Studious, studiously. These words generally make an appearance to describe a special way of avoiding something—apparently in contrast to all the instances of folks accidentally avoiding or shunning people, places, and things.

Stupefied, stupefying. To too many of your readers, these words will only make them think of wizards, wands, and spells.

Stupendous, stupendously. Even though you probably know what they mean, the sounds of these words don't call to mind "amazing," "impressive," "marvelous," or "wondrous." Rather, whether you like it or not, thanks to some shared etymology, you get notes of "stupid."

Stupid, stupidly. Consider adopting this as a personal rule: I'll only use these words in fact sections in employment and criminal cases to quote what someone said.

Subsequent, subsequently. "After" and "later" sound just as good and intelligent. Better, really.

Substantial, substantially. These are fuzzy measures when legal standards require lawyers and judges to employ them. Their meanings aren't made any clearer when writers use them for embellishment, disconnected from whatever moorings formal legal definitions may provide.

Succinct, succinctly. If you have to say this about a writing, you've made it less true by at least one word.

Sudden, suddenly. When you're describing a decision or reversal by opposing counsel or a court, these terms function like a caution flag for a judge to take a hard look at whether the change was as abrupt or unexpected as the writer claims. Sometimes it was, but often signs and warnings were present long before.

Sullied. This word is a fine way to describe a damaged reputation when "tarnished" doesn't sound quite dirty enough.

Super. This word is a very likely overstated way to describe excellence or, as an adverb, to mix things up because you've already used "very" too much. Lawyers—risking calling to mind images of fictional persons with extraordinary abilities—sometimes pair it, as a prefix, with "strong" to describe reasons, justifications, and presumptions. But, no matter how delighted, jubilant, or elated you may be or think someone else should feel, dropping the phrase "super excited" (or the co-opted scientific term "superexcited") on your reader will more likely evoke contrary emotions.

Sure, surely. When using these words, does the writer mean that they are confident about something or have confirmed that it's the case? Or are they only hopeful or cautiously optimistic? What is certain is that every instance of "it's surely the case that" or "feel sure" or "sure to prevail" sounds perilously close to "for sure" or a "sure thing." Some words are better said and left unwritten.

Suspicious, suspiciously. These terms are handy when you're writing a factual account of some mystery or crime to be solved. When they're directed to opposing counsel, they tend toward an understatement because the writer too often seems quite sure of their distrust.

Sweeping, sweepingly. The thing with these kinds of characterizations of others' generalizations and statements is that, like exaggerations, one broad statement seems to beget another, until the court is awash in a sea of generalities.

Swift, swiftly. These terms can be useful if the rest of the writing itself reads like what they say.

Symbolic, symbolically. In legal writing, things have often gotten far afield if you're focusing the court on one thing but telling it that it represents another.

T.

Technical, technically. Technically, holding to a strict or literal interpretation and trying to adhere to the facts and exact meanings are all admirable goals. But employing this overused adverb to tell the court that you're doing so risks making you sound like a bit of a tool.

Tedious, tediously. You may be handling a matter that involved a boring job and the fact that the job wasn't interesting matters. Or maybe it's relevant to a judge to hear how lawyers are feeling about a large document review. Otherwise, it's hard to see how anything productive comes from a writer's reaching for these words to complain to the court.

Telling, tellingly. If you want to, on rare occasions, signal that what comes next puts the lie to the statement that came just before—along the lines of "but the dog didn't bark"—use these terms. But don't stick this sentence adverb in before any point that you're particularly proud of or to alert the judge that you're about to drop a real zinger. (On the other hand, "tells" is an awesome, underused verb.)

Tenable, tenably. These words' opposites (with the "un-") show up more often, and there's no need to increase these terms' rates of appearance when "defensible" and "reasonable" are available. Shorter, it seems, isn't always better.

Terrible, terribly. These terms tend to reflect careless overstatement or snarky understatement. Unless your briefing involves monsters or forces of nature, try another word.

Terrific, terrifically. These words are the stuff of emails and thank-you notes, not legal briefing. And there's nothing good, much less extremely good, about the sound of the adverb form.

Thankless, thanklessly. These words usually describe a task foisted on a junior attorney. Like a document review or a fifty-state survey. The court may not really need to hear it, but descriptions using these terms are usually at least accurate.

The truth is. This is an odd verbal device when you think about it. It implies an unfortunate contrast with the rest of your material, suggesting everything else may be half-truths or lies. And, too often, that may be just what follows this overused throat-clearer.

Theoretical, theoretically. So, you've already used "hypothetically" and "apparently"? Probably. Regardless, reserve these terms for contexts (often scientific or academic) in which there really are no substitutes to choose from because you're contrasting theories and hypotheses with practical applications.

Thin, thinly. These words denote, it seems, the only way that something can be veiled or disguised in a legal context. Like "obvious," these terms throw up at least a yellow flag that perhaps it's not all quite so clear or transparent as the writer suggests.

Thorny, thornily. These are fun words because who doesn't enjoy thinking of rosebushes and spiky vines? But, as with their synonyms, be sure it really is a difficult issue or situation that you're describing before you burden your reader with the account.

Thorough, thoroughly. When writers describe their review, search, or research efforts using these terms, it conveys an impression that maybe it's the exception to the rule or somehow worthy of special praise. Best to use these words only when a quick or superficial effort was a real option that you declined.

Thoughtless, thoughtlessly. In everyday conversation, these words can be gracious alternatives to "careless," "reckless," or "negligent." But those terms involve distinctions and implications in the law that these imprecise (even if more polite) words fail to capture.

Timid, timidly. There may be times to call someone or something out for not being brave or bold. But, if you couldn't stomach substituting "fainthearted," "mousey," or "skittish," take it as a sign that you lack the courage of your convictions on this score, and give these terms a pass.

Tired. This word gets attached to "argument" in briefing that, in making this charge, often itself induces a bit of fatigue.

Tiresome, tiresomely. This is another adjective that centers your briefing on the writer's feelings about or reactions to someone or something. Which may do little but make your reader think that these words might fairly describe the briefing itself and not its subject.

Tolerable, tolerably. When you're not writing about enduring pain or burdens, these terms come off as weaker versions of "passable," "mediocre," or "kind of good"—which isn't saying much.

Too clever by half, too cute by half. These phrases may work at oral argument to take someone down for being excessively or obviously sneaky or clever. But, in writing, these phrases often feel forced, as if the writer had the saying ready to go and wedged it into a scenario where it only halfway fit.

Tortured. Although this word sometimes gets attached to "reasoning," it's hard to get past the word "torture" and all that it conveys.

Toxic, toxically. Although using these terms to describe people rather than chemicals has come into vogue, stick with the words' more traditional applications.

Tragic, tragically. Legal writing is not the place for loose takes on tragedies. Handle these terms with care.

Travesty. Please find another way to express any outrage that you believe you should convey to the court. No judge wants to read another tirade about a "travesty of justice." This word can also—but should never—be used as a verb. If you find yourself writing that "John Smith travestied righteous indignation with his maudlin expressions of outrage," put down the thesaurus, close your eyes, center yourself. And start again.

Tremendous, tremendously. Unless you're dealing with elephants or planets, these terms may as well be a flashing neon sign that reads "I'm exaggerating here."

Tricky, trickily. These words are useful to describe paths or problems but off-putting when describing untrustworthy people. Judges don't expect to read about "cunning," "crafty," "sly," or "wily" folks either.

Trifling, triflingly, trivial, trivially. When writers use these terms to offer assurances about costs or burdens to be borne by an opponent, they risk causing the judge's mind—trained by hard experience—to spring to thoughts of underestimates. And, when writers use these terms to attack an opponents' arguments or concerns, they may be asking for more than they need. There's little to be gained by suggesting that the other side's position is not just wrong but frivolous when its being wrong is good—or, rather, bad—enough.

Trite, tritely. "Overused" and even "clichéd" or "stale" offer a crisper, fresher take than these tired terms.

Troublesome, troublesomely. These terms seem to appear either as a whine or as the punchline in an understated quip (along the lines of "that's not so good" in response to, say, a volcanic eruption). But they're no more helpful in legal writing than their cousins "annoying," "irritating," and "vexatious."

Troubled, troubling, troublingly. These words are great examples of terms with some value in everyday conversation that, when they appear in a brief, don't tell much to the court, which needs to understand what about something should cause (or has caused) anxiety, distress, or worry—and why.

Truly. This adverb is most often used to modify an adjective that is itself an exaggerated description. It functions as a sort of exclamation point in word form—conveying, without adding anything of substance, that you must really mean what you're saying. But it carries the added bonus of suggesting that, without the addition of "truly," whatever adjective or sentiment follows would likely have been false or insincere (think "I am truly sorry"). It's hard to think of an instance in which using "truly" would be helpful or appropriate in legal writing.

Trust me/us, believe me/us. These phrases are generally used to introduce a proposition or statement that the court would be wise to view with suspicion. If you feel the need to include this phrase, think very carefully about whether you should be saying to the judge whatever follows.

Two-bit. Even if something deserves to be called out as cheap, trivial, or worthless, this term is a bit cutting and caustic for a legal brief.

Two-faced. I suppose it's a plus that a lawyer slapping this label on someone in legal writing can't be accused of sugarcoating their language for their opponents while bashing them to the court. But, if the vitriol has built up to the point that this insult has made an appearance, the briefing has probably gone off the rails in any event.

Typical, typically. These are useful terms to describe something as being a good example of a type of thing or person. These are unhelpful terms when used to complain that your opponents or others are acting like their worst selves.

U.

Ubiquitous, ubiquitously. Strictly speaking, these words are limited to something that is everywhere at the same time, but in practice they cover things that are or have become very common. But these ten-cent words don't need to themselves be some of them.

Ultimate, ultimately. What is meant to convey something that is last or final, an endpoint, too often shows up as a fancier way of saying "awesome" or a less fancy way of saying "quintessential." Which are both incorrect and unhelpful. And, if you're looking to describe the best there ever was, on paper this adjective doesn't look any better than "G.O.A.T."—which one hopes we'll never see in legal writing.

Unacceptable, unacceptably. There's no denying these terms' place in the law. But there's a subjective or relative element ("the offer is unacceptably low to us," "the results are unacceptable compared to the benchmarks") that legal writers should keep in mind.

Unaccountable, unaccountably. The responsibility-based meanings of these terms seem to be overtaking the explainable-based meanings. But, even with the former sense of the words, there's a risk of confusing these terms as meaning someone can't justify the actions rather than that they are not required to defend or explain them. That's a lot to account for when there are other terms that can do the same work for less trouble.

Unadorned, unadornedly. These words offer an affected way to describe something as plain or simple—as if the missing embellishment had to land somewhere.

Unarguable, unarguably. Some real words sound like you just made them up out of desperate need in the moment. These are two of them.

Unashamed, unashamedly. Shame may be an important part of the human condition, but it's being asked to do a lot of work centering these terms for acting without guilt, embarrassment, self-consciousness, or doubt. Set aside the shame references, and opt for a more descriptive term for your particular facts.

Unassuming, unassumingly. More words for someone who is modest or unpretentious—not, as they seem to be used (or at least appear alongside) more and more, for something that's "sneaky good." Which, I understand, isn't quite where it needs to be to make it into legal briefing just yet.

Unavailing, unavailingly. These terms have been a long-time favorite of mine. And they certainly roll off the tongue better than "ineffectual," and they're not as overused in legal standards as "futile." But you can't go to this well more than once in a brief.

Unbearable, unbearably. There's no way to say these words without it coming off as a complaint. And an exasperated one at that.

Unbelievable, unbelievably, beyond belief. Is it really? Your opponent's conduct or statements cannot be believed?

Uncanny, uncannily. "Uncanny" is a fun word, and is usually followed by "ability." But it's uncommon enough that some readers will need to stop and think about it. And others will just think of vintage comic books. And the adverb version sounds ridiculous. Steer clear.

Unceremonious, unceremoniously. To those who aren't connoisseurs of synonyms for "rude," these terms may be mistaken for alternatives to "informal" that are just trying too hard.

Unconfirmed. This word describes the first (or larval) stage of most reports, apparently.

Unconstitutional, unconstitutionally. These terms appear all the time in certain kinds of cases. But, in other contexts, it's apparently worth a reminder that they aren't just all-purpose descriptors for anything that a writer or her client thinks is bad or should be universally banned.

Unctuous, unctuously. This is another pair of words that sound a bit like what they mean. But calling your opponent oily or falsely flattering won't sound good to any reader.

Undeniable, undeniably. Lawyers can be a contrarian bunch, and these words invite a challenge. Make sure that what you're describing is really up for it.

Understated, understatedly. In legal briefing, these words are probably appearing only in jest to describe another's writing—which probably isn't overstated but likely is unnecessary.

Undignified, undignifiedly. You hopefully aren't often writing about silly or foolish behavior. If you must, these words can maintain the dignity of your writing, if not your target.

Undistinguished. Insulting something as unworthy of notice or mention feels a bit unbecoming of a legal writer.

Undue, unduly. Such common words in legal standards, and yet so poorly defined. You must use them in many contexts, so give them a rest in all the others.

Unencumbered. Very useful if you're looking to channel Oscar Wilde, telling your reader that the subject "was something of a mystery. So much of what he'd accomplished in life seemed to require that he be quite charming. And yet in public he appeared to be entirely unencumbered by that quality." (That was fun to write.) This is a great word for delivering self-deprecation and insults. And, for that same reason, it's likely to weigh down the tone and quality of your legal writing.

Unequivocal, unequivocally. Two terms that leave no doubt that a lawyer wrote them.

Uneventful, uneventfully. These terms may sometimes be preferable to "nothing (much) happened." Especially if you've already had to say just that a few times, which would be unusual, since lawyers rarely find themselves litigating over (truly) nothing.

Unexplained, unexplainedly. Sometimes these terms refer to a genuine mystery. Other times—as in "what is left unexplained"—they're used to highlight something that the writer believes their opponent cannot explain or justify (to the writer's satisfaction, at least).

Unfair, unfairly. The law is concerned with fairness, and many legal standards in several contexts reflect that and incorporate these terms. But, outside of those situations, you risk coming off as the youth soccer coach who's yelling at the ref if you put too fine a point on your frustration, indignation, or outrage by using these terms. Lay out the facts and circumstances, and let the judge be the first one to call it like it is by name.

Unfathomable, unfathomably. There are many words that describe something as difficult to understand. These, unfortunately, lend themselves to writers trying very hard to sound deep while using terms that are based in six feet of water.

Unflinching, unflinchingly. These words offer a way to describe strong opposition by reference to a game of chicken.

Unhelpful, unhelpfully. Sometimes these words are the best that can be said of something, as plenty of the entries above and below this one illustrate.

Uniform, uniformly. These terms are almost always qualified by "almost" or the like—because, when legal writers can do so accurately, they are happy to discard these words and plainly spell out that something is true in all cases and at all times.

Unimaginable, unimaginably. Many lawyers can imagine a lot of things, whether they'd like to or not. Make sure that what you're referring to really is one of the few things beyond the reach of anyone's imagination.

Uninformed, uninformedly. These terms offer a fine alternative to "ignorant," and they have the added benefit of sounding like what they mean. And, in any event, they come off as less demeaning than most of their synonyms.

Unintelligent, unintelligently. These words may sound fancier, but they're still just as inappropriately insulting as "dumb" or "stupid."

Unintelligible, unintelligibly. Don't mix up these terms with others that describe the merely confusing or disorganized. These words describe something that's truly gobbledygook—which, of course, is itself too technical a term for legal writing.

Uninteresting, uninterestingly. In some fields, "that may be true, but it just isn't interesting" may be a legitimate response to an argument. Law isn't one of them. And so these words don't have much good work to do in legal writing.

Uninterrupted, uninterruptedly. These terms often appear with a kind of negative subtext—suggesting that the reader would've preferred that there had been some interference or intrusion.

Unique, uniquely. These terms are too often misused before "qualified" or "positioned" when someone has strong, but not singular, qualifications or is in a good, but not exclusive, position to perceive or understand something. And, so, stripped of their proper one-of-a-kind meanings, these words have become empty filler.

Universal, universally. These absolute terms often read as more hoped-for than accurately descriptive in legal briefing. If only wishing could make it so.

Unmistakable, unmistakably. Using these words rarely, if you must at all, will lead to crisper writing than sprinkling in too many instances of "there can be no mistaking that" or "make no mistake."

Unmitigated, unmitigatedly. These terms describe a special kind of disaster—in contrast to the mild or well-controlled kind, apparently.

Unnecessary, unnecessarily. Necessity may sometimes be in the eye of the beholder, and so judges seem to read these words a lot in the context of things that a lawyer doesn't want to give or do for his opponent.

Unobtrusive, unobtrusively, inobstrusive, inobstrusively. These words offer a fairly hard-to-miss way to describe something as unnoticeable.

Unparalleled. If you're not writing about the greatest of all time or at least the best there is right now at something, you're overusing this term.

Unprecedented, unprecedentedly. Some decisions by courts have never before been made; some legal issues have never before been faced or decided; and some events have never before happened. But, when faced with those first-time experiences, lawyers often say just that—and then dilute these words' meanings by deploying them in other contexts to describe instances that may be rare or uncommon or momentous but are not previously unknown.

Unqualified, unqualifiedly. Two terms that oddly cut in different directions, either tearing someone down as lacking required education, training, or traits or pumping something up as unencumbered by any limitations or restrictions. Avoid making your reader distinguish which one you mean, and opt for words that fit only one bill or the other.

Unquestionable, unquestionably. Judges may sometimes wonder if a writer has met many lawyers when she reads these terms. But some things aren't open to question, and most judges would probably agree that they don't need to read any more instances of "indisputable" or "indubitably" and will gladly take these words instead.

Unreasonable, unreasonably. Plenty of legal terms of art or standards involve these terms. Outside of those contexts, these words often show up in motions or briefs as code for "he just won't agree with me" or "he refuses to concede his position"—which doesn't really merit its own modifier and doesn't tell a judge much at all about whether and why your opponent should yield.

Unremarkable, unremarkably. You shouldn't often need to deploy such long words to describe something that's not interesting or worthy of note or mention. And maybe you don't need to describe something like that at all.

Unrepresentative, unrepresentatively. These are unwieldy terms, to be sure, but apart from "atypical," the other options ("abnormal," "divergent," "aberrant") carry hints of derision and scorn.

Unruly. There are better ways to convey disorderly conduct that don't inevitably call to mind schoolchildren or uncombed hair.

Unsatisfactory, unsatisfactorily. Along with being a bit clunky, when measured against alternatives like "unacceptable" or "inadequate," these terms carry an overtone of subjectivity that may add an unwelcome or unnecessary element to your argument or position.

Unsightly. This word's relative obscurity doesn't make it any less insulting than "ugly" or "unattractive." Not a problem with buildings and other objects, but a judge may be put off if this is directed at something with feelings.

Unsolicited. This is the word of choice for stiff-arming advice that an attorney or party would rather not hear.

Unsophisticated, unsophisticatedly. "Not complicated" is one thing that can't be said about this seven-syllable adverbial beast.

Unstoppable, unstoppably. These words call to mind either superheroes or immovable objects. And you can prevent that distraction.

Unsupported. This way leads to passive voice. Be better. Be active.

Unsure, unsurely. This adjective is an important alternative to "uncertain" and a decided upgrade from "unconfident." But adding "un-" does little to improve the sound of "surely."

Unswerving. This word depicts a special kind of devotion or loy-alty, one that stays between the lines and doesn't zig or zag.

Untenable, untenably. These words provide a more eloquent way to declare an argument or position a loser, but one that's no more helpful to a judge without more.

Untimely. This is a word to be careful of. It suggests that there is a proper or set time for something. Sometimes there's not. And too often that's when lawyers deploy this.

Untroubled. In a broader context, this word can nicely capture how someone is indifferent—or a sociopath. But, in legal writing, it's a bit too much of an invitation to snark or sarcasm.

Unwieldy, unwieldily. The only virtue of this adverb is that it illustrates its own meaning. And much the same can be said of the only slightly less ungraceful adjective.

Unwitting, unwittingly. I suppose, in some legal contexts, you can always use another way to convey a lack of knowledge, aware-ness, or intent—even one that looks a bit like the middle of "un-willing" shrunk and put on hats.

Unworkable, unworkably. Though a bit clunky, this word fairly describes more than a few legal standards that have been developed over the years.

Unworthy, unworthily. This adjective calls to mind the satirical title of a disgraced knight in medieval times. And the adverb is itself a bit of a disgrace to the English language and raises the ques-tion: How exactly do you act in an unworthy manner?

Unyielding, unyieldingly. In a military history, these words might be used to describe a heroic stand against superior forces or a vicious assault. In legal writing, they're pretty much only used to convey exasperation at an opponent who won't just give up despite how obvious it is to the writer that he should.

Upon. This word sounds good in some Victorian-era poetry. Leave it to the poets, and just use "on."

Uppity. This word carries a connotation you either don't or shouldn't want to convey. If you really need to describe someone as overconfident when they should take it down a notch, try "haughty." But it's hard to imagine why you'd be sharing such a description with a court in any event.

Upset, upsetting. You may enjoy, in informal conversation, the understatement of reacting to something terrible with the wry observation "that's upsetting." Some of us do. But that's not the kind of understatement that you're going for in a motion or brief. And, outside of hostile work environments and a few other factual circumstances where it might matter for a legal standard, the court and your opponent don't need to read about your or your client's emotional reactions.

Urgent, urgently. Describing something using these words is a great way to get most judges to believe that it really isn't. Avoid these descriptors except when recounting how someone acted in a relevant prior event, and, instead, use facts to show, not tell, the court that a matter requires its immediate attention.

Useless, uselessly. Nothing productive comes from using these terms to describe something a judge or opponent did or said. A good rule of thumb is to think of these words as describing themselves for purposes of legal writing and to keep them tucked away in your toolbox unless and until you need to describe a broken or defective device.

Usurped, usurping. Are you litigating a claim to a medieval throne? It'd be neat if you were. But you're probably not, so don't risk distracting your reader with wandering thoughts of political intrigue.

Utilize. This is fairly described as a word that only a lawyer or consultant could love. And that is never meant as a compliment. Use "use."

Utter, utterly. A cousin of "absolutely," but one that calls to mind a part of a cow and should, for that reason, too, be avoided.

V.

Vacuous, vacuously. These terms provide an extravagant way to insult someone as lacking thought or intelligence. Maybe they offer the advantage of assuring that, if you're right, the object of your take-down won't understand it. But "empty-headed" would—because it is so easily understood—leave more of a mark. In any event, you don't need to be swimming in these shallow waters.

Vague, vaguely. Some written words or spoken expressions do lack a clear meaning or reflect a lack of focus or precision in what the writer or speaker is trying to convey. But the same can be said of many instances of writers using these words to disparage their opponents' arguments.

Valiant, valiantly. In a far cry from according an opponent the respect due a noble medieval prince, these terms tend to be bestowed in legal writing like a pat on the head of an eager but bumbling dog.

Valid, validly. Arguments, contracts, and official documents may be valid in ways that matter in legal briefing in many contexts. Faced with all of that, judges may find that reading these terms used more loosely—and often as a backhanded compliment—to bless a point or position as reasonable lies beyond their patience's saturation point.

Vast, vastly. Really big. Extremely broad or extensive. We can't define these words without relying on other words that carry the same shortcoming, and so all these words tell your reader very little useful information or detail.

Vast majority. This phrase offers a more and unnecessarily hyperbolic way of saying "most."

Vast multitude. Are you describing stars in the galaxy? A barbarian horde? No? Then don't use this exaggerated phrase.

Vehement, vehemently. A Martian first studying American legal writing might believe that we must have a rule that, when a legal writer wants to deny something but forgets to include one of these terms, she automatically admits that which she says she rejects.

Verbose. When you read this term in a brief, it's often a good opportunity to reflect on the shared color of pots and kettles.

Verily. A favorite of William Shakespeare. But it's been a while since he was writing. And, even if the word wasn't a bit dated, you shouldn't begin any sentences with this or any other variation of "Truly" or "In complete honesty."

Very limited. A great phrase when just "limited" will not do. Not always unnecessary verbiage. But often it is—maybe even very often.

Very same. When something is extra-identical, this phrase is essential—accept no substitute.

Vexatious, vexatiously. These terms are overused in the contexts in which they're terms of art. No need to risk annoying your reader with loosey-goosey references untethered from any defined legal standards.

Vexed, vexing, vexingly. Aren't we all, from time to time? But, while this sounds better than complaining that you're annoyed or frustrated, it's complaining all the same, and likely to induce the same feeling in your reader.

Villainous, villainously. You're thinking of comic books and superspy films, right? How could you not be? The judge will be. And, while this adverb may look tempting to add as a bucket list item to use once in your career, you really shouldn't.

Violent, violently. Violence and even mayhem are the stuff of criminal and tort law, at the least. Using these terms as essentially metaphorical synonyms for strong but nonviolent disagreement or opposition may not provoke an extreme reaction from a judge who handles matters involving actual physical altercations, but it may not draw positive feedback either.

Virtual, virtually. These terms function as synonyms for the nonliteral sense of "literally" but with the bonus of ambiguity as to whether you're referring to something as essentially but not actually in this universe or to something that's actual in the metaverse. In the online era, better to reserve these terms for references to things that are only computer-generated and not physical.

Vocal, vocally. When a writer reaches for this note, it's usually a signal that she would've preferred silence.

Voluminous, voluminously. These words offer a lengthy way to describe another piece of writing as lengthy.

Voracious, voraciously. These terms apparently only describe an appetite. Which judges will have none of for this five-cent term.

W.

Wacky, wackily. These words are an appropriate way to describe an over-the-top comedy film or a farcical one-act play. Or a court jester. But you can't be calling your opponent or a judge a clown.

Warm, warmly. This sounds nice. Really. But, unless you're writing about temperatures or sweaters, including these terms in a brief is more odd than sweet.

Warranted. If you've somehow hit your quotas of "justified" and "well-founded," using this word may be, you know, warranted.

Warring. This adjective feels like what some English teachers might praise as vivid imagery. But lawyers comparing competing ideas, arguments, or positions to factions or nations in armed conflicts comes off as a bit misguided.

Wary, warily. Not to be (but often will be) confused with "weary." In legal writing, "wary" often shows up where an attorney is warning the court to be careful when considering something an opponent is reporting or advising the court to be skeptical of an opponent's suggestion or representation. It's not a bad word for this job. But legal writers should be mindful of their tone when giving judges advice or warnings. As when reporting an opponent's bad behavior, it is often better just to state the facts and let the judge reach her own conclusion than to tell her how to feel.

Wayward, waywardly. These are fine words if you're briefing a tennis match or a sailing regatta. Or the escapades of early-twenti-eth-century London street urchins.

Weak, weakly. There are more persuasive, less in-your-face ways to say that your opponent's argument or a court's reasoning isn't strong. Like "not persuasive" or "unconvincing."

Weary, wearily, wearying, wearyingly, wearisome, weari-somely. These words are used as a fancy way to say that you're sick of or have been beaten down by a particular dispute. Or sometimes to guess at how the judge is feeling about the progress of the case: "The Court has no doubt grown weary of this seemingly never-ending motion practice." But sharing your mental state or guessing at the judge's is a poor use of the precious real estate in your brief. Save this word for a statement of facts in which it matters that someone was physically or mentally tired.

Weird, weirdly. These words do a lot of good work and don't have to be replaced with "strange," "odd," or "unusual" every time. But limit their use to describing something other than another party, the court, or its rulings.

Well acquainted. This phrase is a powdered-wig-wearing way of saying that someone knows a lot about the case's facts.

Well aware. This phrase is used to describe what the court—or the writer herself or, when she is being accused of knowing better, the writer's opponent—does not just know but really, really knows.

Well deserved. Litigation often gets contentious. And so this phrase more often takes the shade of just deserts and not a celebration of another's good fortune.

Well intentioned. When a judge reads this phrase, she expects that it'll be followed by a "but" and a criticism ("naive," "failed," "weak," "harmful"—the list goes on). And it's what follows the "but" that'll stick with the court; what comes before doesn't soften the blow or reduce the sting.

Whimsical, whimsically. These terms are more fitting for describing a fairy wonderland than another lawyer's positions or arguments. And it'd be funny (in a strange way) to come across legal arguments that really are full of whimsy.

Whining, whiny. One shudders to think where the written exchanges in a matter would have to go before you'd use these terms in formal legal writing. Also, "I know you are but what am I?" comes to mind.

Wholesale. This adjective offers a way to make clear that you're not referring to retail destruction or resale changes.

Wicked, wickedly. Litigation can be heated. But you should always be able to keep matters outside the realm of fairytale villains.

Wide-eyed. And bushy-tailed? The idiom is actually "bright-eyed and bushy-tailed." But all these terms are too squirrely for formal legal writing.

Widely. Lawyers' word of choice to punch up their account of how accepted, recognized, or used their favored proposition or authority or device is by tagging it with this signal that amounts to more than a few but less than all people. But that's not really saying a lot. Offer some more detailed measure if you can, because, if you don't, your reader will likely assume that you can't.

Wild. In some regions, you may be briefing cases about mustangs, feral cats, or vermin. Outside of that context, this word just risks sounding kind of mean or inappropriate.

Wildly. This adverb is used to tell a court that something is not just, for example, inconsistent—or (much more positively) successful or effective, or (somewhat less so) optimistic—but extremely so. That might work at times at oral argument. On the written page, this intensifier only lends itself to making your argument come off as exaggerated or ambiguous or, at best, imprecise.

Willful, willfully, wilful, wilfully. These terms get enough play in tort and criminal cases, with sometimes unclear line-drawing with their "reckless" and "knowing" cousins. Save them for those contexts—and leave the one-*l* spellings to our colleagues across the pond.

Wise, wisely. In modern legal writing, judges don't read these terms in connection with sound advice or sage counsel but rather to express smug approval for an opponent's giving up something (an argument, a fight, their rights). More often than not, you may want to abandon that negative usage of these otherwise complimentary terms.

Woeful, woefully. Contemporary legal writers seem to feel that charges of inadequacy can't be made without taking on one of these words. But these terms themselves come off as more befitting of describing a Dickensian pauper's plight.

Wonderful, wonderfully. When employed without irony, these terms are quite nice but—unless you're describing the Northern Lights or some other natural phenomenon or landmark—a little too casual for legal writing.

Worried, worriedly, worrisome, worrisomely, worrying, worryingly. Worrying about someone or something reflects concern, care, or even compassion. When that's often absent amid conflicting legal arguments, these terms instead reflect criticism or condescension, and a writer's worry would be better directed to whether that's a good look before the court.

Worst-case. Is it really? We have all fallen prey to the temptation to conflate the bad or maybe even the really bad with the "most bad" of all possible or foreseeable scenarios. If you're not writing about earthquakes, shark attacks, or Category 5 tornados or hurricanes, you're probably exaggerating.

Worthless, worthlessly. These words have positive value for describing currency or assets, but they amount to a net negative when applied to people and their intangible assets. No court is going to give you a declaration of someone's essential worth as a human being, and you may hurt your own standing with the judge if you seem to be asking for one.

Worthwhile. When you describe some effort or spending using this term, it's hard to avoid sounding presumptuous, as if the writer is decreeing whether it's worthy of his time or effort.

Wretched, wretchedly. I have a soft spot for these words. I just like how they sound. But you shouldn't describe any person this way in a legal brief, and it's hard to see why you'd need to describe feeling unhappy. And, if you're describing a rundown or poor-quality thing or condition, you're probably better off being more descriptive.

Wrong, wrongly. When used to mean "incorrect" or "incorrectly," those alternative words read better on the page and don't carry the risk of being confused with another meaning. When used to convey a moral failing or "wrong," using these words risks stripping them of their force through overuse. And, for some reason, in that context, they seem to always invite their friends "just" or "demonstrably" along, like some kind of magnetic attraction.

Wrought. This adjective is a pretty overstated way of saying carefully made. You may enjoy it from some of your favorite lines in the Scottish Play or verses in the King James Bible. But it doesn't belong in post-1611 legal writing.

X.

Xenophobic. Fancy? Technical-sounding? Absolutely. But what are your other choices? "Alien-hating"? "Foreigner-disliking"? Sometimes you have no alternative. If you need a word to factually describe someone who is prejudiced against those from another country, this five-cent (or maybe ten-cent?—it starts with an *x*!) word is, improbably, the way to go.

Y.

Yearning, yearningly. Reports of intense longing should be confined to your beach reading.

Yeoman. Unless you need to describe someone working in a royal or noble household, this shows up as "yeoman's work" or "yeoman's job." But that's a lot of heavy lifting—including for your readers who may not be familiar with these relatively obscure phrases—just to say someone "did hard work" or "put in good effort."

Yet another. This phrase is a signal to the court that you're very frustrated and weary of what your opponent has or has not been doing. Like any cry of exasperation, this should be used sparingly.

Yielding. Standing alone (without "high-" or "low-" for company), this word is lost in the shadow of its opposite and will just trip your readers up.

Youthful. It's hard to think of this word without hearing "exuberance" in the next moment. There may be some situations in legal writing in which you must describe a person or their conduct this way, but it's hard to imagine too many that wouldn't come off as your condescendingly patting the attorney or party in question on the head.

Z.

Zealous, zealously. A lawyer may find herself discussing the ethical standard for how to represent a client and forced to refer to that formal standard by name or to measure some conduct against it. Otherwise, if a lawyer—in her enthusiasm to advance her client's position—uses these terms to refer to her own conduct (to bolster why it's commendable) or opposing counsel's behavior (to denigrate it), something's likely gone awry.

Bonus Material

Some adjectives and adverbs didn't quite merit their own entries but can be helpfully categorized into lists based on a shared reason that legal writers should use each of them less often or not at all. As bonus material, I've collected those lists in this final section of the book, along with the list (without explanations) of the Top 50 to Avoid.

Adverbs whose company even adjectives prefer not to keep

- Advisedly
- Appealingly
- Awesomely
- Bindingly
- Bloodily
- Boringly
- Brashly
- Circumstantially
- Clarifyingly
- Colloquially
- Conciliatorily
- Conflictedly
- Conflictingly
- Conspiratorially
- Conspiringly
- Constrainedly
- Contemplatively
- Contemporarily
- Controversially
- Cumbersomely

- Cutely
- Daffily
- Daintily
- Deceivingly
- Depravedly
- Detestably
- Deviously
- Dexterously
- Disconcertedly
- Disconcertingly
- Discretionarily
- Economically
- Embarrassedly
- Embarrassingly
- Emptily
- Enlighteningly
- Evilly
- Exaggeratedly
- Exaltedly
- Excellently
- Familiarly
- Fancily
- Fancifully
- Filthily
- Fishily
- Flakily
- Flightily
- Flintily
- Freakily
- Frighteningly
- Funkily
- Gaudily
- Grouchily
- Guiltily
- Haughtily
- Headily
- Illusorily
- Imaginarily
- Impertinently
- Incredulously
- Indestructibly
- Irreverently
- Laudatorily
- Murkily
- Nastily
- Nervily
- Numbly
- Optionally
- Overlappingly
- Overweeningly
- Perceptibly
- Peskily
- Pettily
- Phonily
- Precedingly
- Prettily

- Prevalently
- Prosperously
- Punchily
- Punily
- Quirkily
- Quizzically
- Reservedly
- Restrainedly
- Resultingly
- Revolutionarily
- Sacrificially
- Scarily
- Scoundrelly
- Smarmily
- Smugly
- Sneakily
- Sophisticatedly
- Speculatively
- Speechlessly
- Speedily
- Spiritedly
- Stably
- Standardly
- Startlingly
- Stealthily
- Steeply
- Stonily
- Stoutly
- Straightly
- Tackily
- Tamely
- Tastily
- Tiringly
- Toughly
- Transformationally
- Tribally
- Uncivilly
- Uncouthly
- Unfamiliarly
- Unfoundedly
- Ungroundedly
- Uninterestedly
- Unitedly
- Unoriginally
- Unreadably
- Unrealizably
- Unrelatedly
- Unreliably
- Unremittingly
- Unrestrainedly
- Unrestrictedly
- Unstably
- Unusably
- Vilely
- Vulgarly
- Wondrously

Fancy words you're not sure you know (or want to know) the meanings of

- Adroit, adroitly
- Aggrandized, aggrandizing
- Apposite, appositely, appositional, appositionally
- Artless, artlessly
- Avaricious, avariciously
- Befouled, befouling
- Bemused, bemusing, bemusingly
- Bespoke
- Boorish, boorishly
- Bourgeois
- Bowdlerized, bowdlerizing
- Callow, callowly
- Caustic, caustically
- Chimeric, chimerically
- Circumlocutory
- Complementarily
- Complimentarily
- Conflated, conflating
- Confluent, confluently
- Consternated, consternating
- Contemplative
- Continuingly
- Contrived, contrivedly
- Cryptic, cryptically
- Deigning
- Demure, demurred, demurring, demurringly
- Didactic, didactically
- Diffident, diffidently
- Disputatious, disputatiously
- Dissembling, dissemblingly
- Eclectic, eclectically
- Ecumenical, ecumenically
- Edifying, edifyingly
- Effervescent, effervescently
- Effusive, effusively
- Elucidating
- Enervated

- Enervating
- Ephemeral, ephemerally
- Epitomic, epitomical
- Esoteric, esoterically
- Euphemistic, euphemistically
- Exuberant, exuberantly
- Exultant, exulting, exultingly
- Facetious, facetiously
- Fatuous, fatuously
- Feckless, fecklessly
- Felicitous, felicitously
- Flummoxed
- Fraught, freighted
- Garish, garishly
- Garrulous, garrulously
- Gauche, gauchely
- Gaudy
- Genial, genially
- Genteel, genteelly
- Germane, germanely
- Hallowed
- Haughty
- Hubristic, hubristically
- Illusory
- Impertinent
- Laudatory
- Mendacious, mendaciously
- Misbegotten
- Myopic, myopically
- Nefarious, nefariously
- Nihilistic, nihilistically
- Nugatory
- Odious, odiously
- Omnipotent, omnipotently
- Omnipresent
- Omniscient, omnisciently
- Ontological, ontologically
- Overweening
- Overwrought
- Parochial, parochially
- Pecuniary, pecuniarily
- Pensive, pensively
- Perturbed, perturbing, perturbingly
- Petulant, petulantly
- Piquant, piquantly
- Polemic, polemically
- Precursory

- Prevalent
- Primordial, primordially
- Proletarian
- Propinquitous
- Provincial, provincially
- Pugnacious, pugnaciously
- Purposive, purposively
- Quizzical
- Recursive, recursively
- Redoubtable, redoubtably
- Reductive, reductively
- Reproachful, reproachfully
- Risible, risibly
- Rockily
- Rueful, ruefully
- Sardonic, sardonically
- Solicitous, solicitously
- Sophistic, sophistically
- Sporadic, sporadically
- Subjugated, subjugating
- Supercilious, superciliously
- Symbiotic, symbiotically
- Tautological, tautologically
- Teleological, teleologically
- Transformative
- Truncated
- Verminous, verminy
- Vitiating
- Vituperative
- Winnowed, winnowing

Go-to choices when you get points for each letter or syllable you use

- Annihilative
- Belligerent, belligerently
- Ceremonious, ceremoniously
- Circumlocutorily
- Circumnavigated, circumnavigating
- Egomaniacal, egomaniacally

- Formalistic, formalistically
- Reactionary, reactionarily

- Recapitulated
- Undistinguishably

Lawyerly words to use only under legal obligation or duress

- Adjudicated
- Adverse, adversely
- Annulled, annulling
- Anticipatory, anticipatorily
- Bifurcated
- Binding
- Bright-line
- Circumstantial
- Conciliatory
- Contravened, contravening
- Discretionary
- Interlocutory
- Invalidated, invalidating
- Involuntary, involuntarily
- Lascivious, lasciviously
- Legalistic, legalistically
- Lewd, lewdly
- Licentious, licentiously
- Litigious, litigiously
- Multiplicitous, multiplicitously
- Negated, negating
- Negligent, negligently
- Perjured, perjurious, perjuriously
- Precedential, precedentially
- Preclusive, preclusively
- Quashed
- Reciprocal, reciprocally
- Stipulated
- Tortious, tortiously
- Verified
- Vicarious, vicariously
- Void
- Voidable
- Volitional, volitionally

Sentence adverbs that no one will miss

- Actually
- Apparently
- Basically
- Briefly
- Certainly
- Clearly
- Conceivably
- Confidentially
- Correlatively
- Curiously
- Evidently
- Frankly
- Honestly
- Hopefully
- Hypothetically
- Ideally
- Incidentally
- Interestingly
- Ironically
- Naturally
- Predictably
- Presumably
- Regrettably
- Remarkably
- Similarly
- Specifically
- Strangely
- Surprisingly
- Technically
- Thankfully
- Theoretically
- Truthfully
- Ultimately
- Unfortunately

Words to give your writing the sound and feel of a technical guide or instruction manual

- Adulterated
- Assimilated, assimilating, assimilative
- Bilateral, bilaterally
- Centralized
- Conjunctive, conjunctively
- Correlative
- Coterminous, coterminously
- Debilitated, debilitating, debilitatingly
- Disjunctive, disjunctively

- Duplicative
- Formulaic, formulaically
- Multilateral, multilaterally
- Operational, operationally
- Operative, operatively
- Oppositional, oppositionally
- Reiterative, reiteratively
- Qualitative, qualitatively
- Quantitative, quantitatively
- Situational, situationally
- Unadulterated

Words you never thought you'd see in a brief—or need to

- Adorable, adorably
- Angst-ridden
- Angsty
- Awesome
- Ballyhooed
- Bamboozled, bamboozling
- Bedazzled
- Bedeviled, bedeviling
- Bloody
- Cute
- Daffy
- Daft, daftly
- Dainty
- Dazzling, dazzlingly
- Demented, dementedly
- Dim, dimly
- Dimwitted, dimwittedly
- Egotistical, egotistically
- Fabled
- Fabulous, fabulously
- Fishy
- Flailing
- Flaky
- Flighty
- Flinty
- Freaky
- Funky
- Ghoulish, ghoulishly
- Gnawing, gnawingly
- Grungy, grungily

- Hoodwinked
- Hysterical, hysterically
- Impotent, impotently
- Infernal, infernally
- Janky
- Juicy
- Kitschy
- Loony
- Loopy
- Naked, nakedly
- Ornery
- Parasitic, parasitically
- Peevish, peevishly
- Persnickety
- Pesky
- Pesty
- Petty
- Phony
- Punchy
- Puny
- Quirky
- Running
- Savage, savagely
- Scrawny
- Screechy
- Shrewish
- Shrill, shrilly
- Slovenly
- Smarmy
- Sneaky
- Speechless
- Spoiled
- Swimmingly
- Tacky
- Tickled
- Tiny
- Tribal
- Unbridled
- Venomous
- Wobbly

Top 50 to Avoid (just the list)

1. Absolute, absolutely
2. Absurd, absurdly
3. Actual, actually
4. Adequate, adequately
5. Almost
6. Always
7. Apparent, apparently
8. Arbitrary, arbitrarily
9. Baseless, baselessly
10. Blatant, blatantly
11. Certainly
12. Clear, clearly
13. Complete, completely
14. Critical, critically
15. Demonstrable, demonstrably
16. Egregious, egregiously
17. Excessive, excessively
18. False, falsely, fraudulent, fraudulently
19. Frivolous, frivolously
20. General, generally
21. Genuine, genuinely
22. Gross, grossly
23. Groundless, groundlessly
24. Incredible, incredibly
25. Indeed
26. Indisputable, indisputably, undisputed, undisputedly
27. Literal, literally
28. Many
29. Mere, merely
30. Meritless, meritlessly
31. Mistaken, mistakenly
32. Necessary, necessarily
33. Needless, needlessly
34. Never
35. Obvious, obviously
36. Ostensible, ostensibly
37. Particularly
38. Plain, plainly
39. Rather
40. Readily
41. Really
42. Remarkable, remarkably
43. Seeming, seemingly
44. Serious, seriously
45. Simply
46. Supposed, supposedly
47. Total, totally
48. Undoubted, undoubtedly
49. Very
50. Wholly

Acknowledgments

My thanks begin with my brilliant, talented, beautiful, generous, caring wife Leigha Simonton. She has supported me in this project from the beginning, as she has in everything else in our personal and professional realms. I'm proud to say that Leigha and I have been married—and best friends—since a young enough age that the last thing of any note that I accomplished without a lot of help or support from her was graduating from college. In this instance, she became all the more excited about the book after I did the proof-of-concept work to persuade her (and me) that my idea could be more than a long bar journal article. And Leigha's inspired suggestion late in my writing process gifted us with the book's title—and proved that genius ideas are often elegant in their simplicity. She explained that she just thought about what my complete draft manuscript was about and that it was "bad words."

My love and thanks to our kids as well. They have been supportive of my book-writing efforts and excited that I'll be a published author, even though they are not (and may never be) legal writers.

I am forever indebted to my friend and law school classmate Professor Noah Messing for offering his insights on how to structure the book—there might be no Top 50 list if we'd not talked—and a generous introduction to my fantastic editor Carol McGeehan.

Carol has been a great mentor and cheerleader for this book from the first time that we talked. And the final product is better beyond measure based on her thoughtful comments and suggestions. I feel so fortunate to have been able to connect with Carol and, with her championing the project, to have Carolina Academic Press take the book on. This is my first book publishing experience, but I cannot imagine a better group of people to be working with.

And a big thank you to Margarita Coale for her invaluable assistance and counsel in getting my relationship with CAP off to the best possible start.

I am so grateful to several friends who, along the way, have offered me their time and attention to serve as sounding boards for my ideas and to read drafts and offer their reactions, insights, recommendations, and suggested edits. And, more generally, I have learned from many lawyers and judges whom I've been privileged to work with and, early on, to clerk for. They've helped me along the way in my lifelong quest to improve and refine my own writing.

My thanks to my former law partner Glen Nager for blessing my dropping both his name and his no-footnote rule in my Introduction—and suggesting that I was somehow the one being generous in doing so.

I could not have made it in my career, in large part, through writing or have ever come up with this book were it not for fantastic English, journalism, and writing teawchers in high school, college, and law school who shared their love of language, grammar, punctuation, and editing with me.

And, going back to the beginning for me, I feel blessed that my loving parents Joe and Julie and sister Bridget supported and encouraged me when it became clear early on that any verbal talents I had would far outshine anything I could ever manage in a sporting arena—or, probably, just about anywhere else.

Finally, to be clear, the views and opinions in this book are my own as the author and do not necessarily represent the views or opinions of any court or judicial organization or any other judge.

Alphabetical Table

Where to Find the Entry for Each Word, Phrase, Rhetorical Device, and Punctuation Mark in this Book

In this table	In this book
Bonus (Adverbs whose company)	**Bonus Material** (Adverbs whose company even adjectives prefer not to keep)
Bonus (Fancy words)	**Bonus Material** (Fancy words you're not sure you know (or want to know) the meanings of)
Bonus (Go-to choices)	**Bonus Material** (Go-to choices when you get points for each letter or syllable you use)
Bonus (Lawyerly words)	**Bonus Material** (Lawyerly words to use only under legal obligation or duress)
Bonus (Sentence adverbs)	**Bonus Material** (Sentence adverbs that no one will miss)
Bonus (Words to give your writing)	**Bonus Material** (Words to give your writing the sound and feel of a technical guide or instruction manual)
Bonus (Words you never thought)	**Bonus Material** (Words you never thought you'd see in a brief—or need to)
More Words	**More Words and Phrases to Use Less or Not at All**
Top 50	**Top 50 to Avoid**

Abashed	More Words
Abashedly	More Words
Abated	More Words
Abating	More Words
Aberrant	More Words
Aberrantly	More Words
Abhorrent	More Words
Abhorrently	More Words
Abject	More Words
Abjectly	More Words
Abjuratory	More Words
Abjured	More Words
Abjuring	More Words
Able	More Words
Ably	More Words
Abnegated	More Words
Abnegating	More Words
Abnormal	More Words
Abnormally	More Words
Abolished	More Words
Abolishing	More Words
Aborted	More Words
Abortive	More Words
Abortively	More Words
Abrasive	More Words

Abrasively	More Words
Abrogated	More Words
Abrogating	More Words
Abrupt	More Words
Abruptly	More Words
Absolute	Top 50
Absolutely	Top 50
Absorbed	More Words
Absorbedly	More Words
Abstemious	More Words
Abstemiously	More Words
Abstract	More Words
Abstractly	More Words
Abstruse	More Words
Abstrusely	More Words
Absurd	Top 50
Absurdly	Top 50
Abundant	More Words
Abundantly	More Words
Accidental	More Words
Accidentally	More Words
Accurate	More Words
Accurately	More Words
Acerbic	More Words
Acerbically	More Words

Acrid	More Words
Acridly	More Words
Active	More Words
Actively	More Words
Actual	Top 50
Actually	Top 50, Bonus (Sentence Adverbs)
Ad hoc	More Words
Ad hominem	More Words
Ad nauseam	More Words
Adamant	More Words
Adamantly	More Words
Additional	More Words
Additionally	More Words
Addled	More Words
Adequate	Top 50
Adequately	Top 50
Adjudicated	Bonus (Lawyerly Words)
Adjunct	More Words
Adjunctly	More Words
Adorable	Bonus (Words You Never Thought)
Adorably	Bonus (Words You Never Thought)
Adroit	Bonus (Fancy Words)
Adroitly	Bonus (Fancy Words)
Adulterated	Bonus (Words To Give Your Writing)
Adverse	Bonus (Lawyerly Words)

Adversely	Bonus (Lawyerly Words)
Advisedly	Bonus (Adverbs Whose Company)
Aforementioned	More Words
Aggrandized	Bonus (Fancy Words)
Aggrandizing	Bonus (Fancy Words)
Aggravated	More Words
Aggravatedly	More Words
Aggravating	More Words
Aggravatingly	More Words
Aggressive	More Words
Aggressively	More Words
Agonizing	More Words
Agonizingly	More Words
Aimless	More Words
Aimlessly	More Words
Alarming	More Words
Alarmingly	More Words
Almost	Top 50
Always	Top 50
Amazing	More Words
Amazingly	More Words
Ambiguous	More Words
Ambiguously	More Words
Ambivalent	More Words
Ambivalently	More Words

Ample	More Words
Amplified	More Words
Amply	More Words
Analogous	More Words
Analogously	More Words
Angst-ridden	Bonus (Words You Never Thought)
Angsty	Bonus (Words You Never Thought)
Annihilative	Bonus (Go-To Choices)
Annoyed	More Words
Annoyedly	More Words
Annoying	More Words
Annoyingly	More Words
Annulled	Bonus (Lawyerly Words)
Annulling	Bonus (Lawyerly Words)
Anticipatorily	Bonus (Lawyerly Words)
Anticipatory	Bonus (Lawyerly Words)
Antiquated	More Words
Antiquatedly	More Words
Antithetical	More Words
Antithetically	More Words
Apocryphal	More Words
Apocryphally	More Words
Appalled	More Words
Appalling	More Words
Appallingly	More Words

Apparent	Top 50
Apparently	Top 50, Bonus (Sentence Adverbs)
Appealingly	Bonus (Adverbs Whose Company)
Apposite	Bonus (Fancy Words)
Appositely	Bonus (Fancy Words)
Appositional	Bonus (Fancy Words)
Appositionally	Bonus (Fancy Words)
Approximate	More Words
Approximately	More Words
Apt	More Words
Aptly	More Words
Arbitrarily	Top 50
Arbitrary	Top 50
Arcane	More Words
Arcanely	More Words
Archaic	More Words
Archaically	More Words
Argue	More Words
Arguendo	More Words
Argumentative	More Words
Argumentatively	More Words
Arrogant	More Words
Arrogantly	More Words
Artful	More Words
Artfully	More Words

Artless	Bonus (Fancy Words)
Artlessly	Bonus (Fancy Words)
Ashamed	More Words
Ashamedly	More Words
Asinine	More Words
Asininely	More Words
Assert	More Words
Assiduous	More Words
Assiduously	More Words
Assimilated	Bonus (Words To Give Your Writing)
Assimilating	Bonus (Words To Give Your Writing)
Assimilative	Bonus (Words To Give Your Writing)
Astonishing	More Words
Astonishingly	More Words
Attenuated	More Words
Attenuating	More Words
Avaricious	Bonus (Fancy Words)
Avariciously	Bonus (Fancy Words)
Awesome	Bonus (Words You Never Thought)
Awesomely	Bonus (Adverbs Whose Company)
Awful	More Words
Awfully	More Words
Awkward	More Words
Awkwardly	More Words
Backward	More Words

Baffled	More Words
Baffling	More Words
Bafflingly	More Words
Bald	More Words
Bald-faced	More Words
Baldly	More Words
Ballyhooed	Bonus (Words You Never Thought)
Bamboozled	Bonus (Words You Never Thought)
Bamboozling	Bonus (Words You Never Thought)
Banal	More Words
Banally	More Words
Bare	More Words
Barely	More Words
Baseless	Top 50
Baselessly	Top 50
Basic	More Words
Basically	More Words, Bonus (Sentence Adverbs)
Bastardized	More Words
Bedazzled	Bonus (Words You Never Thought)
Bedeviled	Bonus (Words You Never Thought)
Bedeviling	Bonus (Words You Never Thought)
Befouled	Bonus (Fancy Words)
Befouling	Bonus (Fancy Words)
Befuddled	More Words
Befuddling	More Words

Befuddlingly	More Words
Begrudged	More Words
Begrudging	More Words
Begrudgingly	More Words
Belied	More Words
Believable	More Words
Believably	More Words
Believe me/us	More Words
Belligerent	Bonus (Go-To Choices)
Belligerently	Bonus (Go-To Choices)
Belying	More Words
Bemused	Bonus (Fancy Words)
Bemusing	Bonus (Fancy Words)
Bemusingly	Bonus (Fancy Words)
Besotted	More Words
Besotting	More Words
Bespoke	Bonus (Fancy Words)
Bewildered	More Words
Bewilderedly	More Words
Bewildering	More Words
Bewilderingly	More Words
Beyond belief	More Words
Beyond peradventure	More Words
Bifurcated	Bonus (Lawyerly Words)
Bilateral	Bonus (Words To Give Your Writing)

Bilaterally	Bonus (Words To Give Your Writing)
Binding	Bonus (Lawyerly Words)
Bindingly	Bonus (Adverbs Whose Company)
Bitter	More Words
Bitterly	More Words
Bizarre	More Words
Bizarrely	More Words
Blatant	Top 50
Blatantly	Top 50
Blinding	More Words
Blindingly	More Words
Blinkered	More Words
Blissful	More Words
Blissfully	More Words
Bloodily	Bonus (Adverbs Whose Company)
Bloodsucking	More Words
Bloody	Bonus (Words You Never Thought)
Bluff	More Words
Bluffly	More Words
Blunt	More Words
Bluntly	More Words
Boldfaced	More Words
Bonkers	More Words
Boorish	Bonus (Fancy Words)
Boorishly	Bonus (Fancy Words)

Boringly	Bonus (Adverbs Whose Company)
Boundless	More Words
Boundlessly	More Words
Bourgeois	Bonus (Fancy Words)
Bowdlerized	Bonus (Fancy Words)
Bowdlerizing	Bonus (Fancy Words)
Brashly	Bonus (Adverbs Whose Company)
Brassbound	More Words
Brazen	More Words
Brazenly	More Words
Breathless	More Words
Breathlessly	More Words
Briefly	Bonus (Sentence Adverbs)
Bright-line	Bonus (Lawyerly Words)
Brilliant	More Words
Brilliantly	More Words
Broad	More Words
Broadly	More Words
Broad-ranging	More Words
Bullish	More Words
Bullishly	More Words
Cagey	More Words
Cagily	More Words
Callow	Bonus (Fancy Words)
Callowly	Bonus (Fancy Words)

Capricious	More Words
Capriciously	More Words
Caustic	Bonus (Fancy Words)
Caustically	Bonus (Fancy Words)
Cautious	More Words
Cautiously	More Words
Cavalier	More Words
Cavalierly	More Words
Ceaseless	More Words
Ceaselessly	More Words
Centralized	Bonus (Words To Give Your Writing)
Ceremonious	Bonus (Go-To Choices)
Ceremoniously	Bonus (Go-To Choices)
Certainly	Top 50, Bonus (Sentence Adverbs)
Chaotic	More Words
Chaotically	More Words
Charily	More Words
Charitable	More Words
Charitably	More Words
Chary	More Words
Cheekily	More Words
Cheeky	More Words
Chimeric	Bonus (Fancy Words)
Chimerically	Bonus (Fancy Words)
Churlish	More Words

Churlishly	More Words
Circular	More Words
Circularly	More Words
Circumlocutorily	Bonus (Go-To Choices)
Circumlocutory	Bonus (Fancy Words)
Circumnavigated	Bonus (Go-To Choices)
Circumnavigating	Bonus (Go-To Choices)
Circumstantial	Bonus (Lawyerly Words)
Circumstantially	Bonus (Adverbs Whose Company)
Civil	More Words
Civilly	More Words
Clarifyingly	Bonus (Adverbs Whose Company)
Clear	Top 50
Clearly	Top 50, Bonus (Sentence Adverbs)
Clever	More Words
Cleverest	More Words
Cleverly	More Words
Clumsily	More Words
Clumsy	More Words
Coincident	More Words
Coincidental	More Words
Coincidentally	More Words
Colloquially	Bonus (Adverbs Whose Company)
Colorful	More Words
Colorfully	More Words

Colossal	More Words
Colossally	More Words
Commonly	More Words
Compelling	More Words
Compellingly	More Words
Competent	More Words
Competently	More Words
Complementarily	Bonus (Fancy Words)
Complete	Top 50
Completely	Top 50
Complicated	More Words
Complicatedly	More Words
Complicating	More Words
Complimentarily	Bonus (Fancy Words)
Compunctious	More Words
Conceivable	More Words
Conceivably	More Words, Bonus (Sentence Adverbs)
Concerning	More Words
Concerningly	More Words
Conciliatorily	Bonus (Adverbs Whose Company)
Conciliatory	Bonus (Lawyerly Words)
Conclusory	More Words
Concomitant	More Words
Concomitantly	More Words
Concrete	More Words

Concretely	More Words
Concurrent	More Words
Concurrently	More Words
Condescending	More Words
Condescendingly	More Words
Confidentially	Bonus (Sentence Adverbs)
Conflated	Bonus (Fancy Words)
Conflating	Bonus (Fancy Words)
Conflictedly	Bonus (Adverbs Whose Company)
Conflictingly	Bonus (Adverbs Whose Company)
Confluent	Bonus (Fancy Words)
Confluently	Bonus (Fancy Words)
Confounded	More Words
Confoundedly	More Words
Confounding	More Words
Confoundingly	More Words
Confused	More Words
Confusedly	More Words
Confusing	More Words
Confusingly	More Words
Conjectural	More Words
Conjecturally	More Words
Conjunctive	Bonus (Words To Give Your Writing)
Conjunctively	Bonus (Words To Give Your Writing)
Conscious	More Words

Consciously	More Words
Consequent	More Words
Consequential	More Words
Consequentially	More Words
Consequently	More Words
Conservative	More Words
Conservatively	More Words
Conspicuous	More Words
Conspicuously	More Words
Conspiratorially	Bonus (Adverbs Whose Company)
Conspiringly	Bonus (Adverbs Whose Company)
Constant	More Words
Constantly	More Words
Consternated	Bonus (Fancy Words)
Consternating	Bonus (Fancy Words)
Constrainedly	Bonus (Adverbs Whose Company)
Constructive	More Words
Constructively	More Words
Contemplative	Bonus (Fancy Words)
Contemplatively	Bonus (Adverbs Whose Company)
Contemporaneous	More Words
Contemporaneously	More Words
Contemporarily	Bonus (Adverbs Whose Company)
Contemptible	More Words
Contemptibly	More Words

Contemptuous	More Words
Contemptuously	More Words
Contend	More Words
Contentious	More Words
Contentiously	More Words
Contingent	More Words
Contingently	More Words
Continuingly	Bonus (Fancy Words)
Contravened	Bonus (Lawyerly Words)
Contravening	Bonus (Lawyerly Words)
Contrived	Bonus (Fancy Words)
Contrivedly	Bonus (Fancy Words)
Controversially	Bonus (Adverbs Whose Company)
Controverted	More Words
Controvertible	More Words
Contumacious	More Words
Contumaciously	More Words
Convincing	More Words
Convincingly	More Words
Correlative	Bonus (Words To Give Your Writing)
Correlatively	Bonus (Sentence Adverbs)
Coterminous	Bonus (Words To Give Your Writing)
Coterminously	Bonus (Words To Give Your Writing)
Cowardly	More Words
Craftily	More Words

Crafty	More Words
Craven	More Words
Cravenly	More Words
Crazed	More Words
Crazedly	More Words
Crazily	More Words
Crazy	More Words
Credible	More Words
Credibly	More Words
Credulous	More Words
Credulously	More Words
Critical	Top 50
Critically	Top 50
Crushing	More Words
Crushingly	More Words
Cryptic	Bonus (Fancy Words)
Cryptically	Bonus (Fancy Words)
Cumbersomely	Bonus (Adverbs Whose Company)
Curiously	Bonus (Sentence Adverbs)
Curmudgeonly	More Words
Cursorily	More Words
Cursory	More Words
Cute	Bonus (Words You Never Thought)
Cutely	Bonus (Adverbs Whose Company)
Daffily	Bonus (Adverbs Whose Company)

Daffy	Bonus (Words You Never Thought)
Daft	Bonus (Words You Never Thought)
Daftly	Bonus (Words You Never Thought)
Daintily	Bonus (Adverbs Whose Company)
Dainty	Bonus (Words You Never Thought)
Damning	More Words
Damningly	More Words
Dastardly	More Words
Daunted	More Words
Dauntedly	More Words
Daunting	More Words
Dauntingly	More Words
Dauntless	More Words
Dauntlessly	More Words
Dazzling	Bonus (Words You Never Thought)
Dazzlingly	Bonus (Words You Never Thought)
Deafening	More Words
Deafeningly	More Words
Debatable	More Words
Debatably	More Words
Debilitated	Bonus (Words To Give Your Writing)
Debilitating	Bonus (Words To Give Your Writing)
Debilitatingly	Bonus (Words To Give Your Writing)
Deceivingly	Bonus (Adverbs Whose Company)
Decent	More Words

Decently	More Words
Decimated	More Words
Defiant	More Words
Defiantly	More Words
Deficient	More Words
Deficiently	More Words
Definite	More Words
Definitely	More Words
Definitive	More Words
Definitively	More Words
Deigning	Bonus (Fancy Words)
Deleterious	More Words
Deleteriously	More Words
Deliberate	More Words
Deliberately	More Words
Demented	Bonus (Words You Never Thought)
Dementedly	Bonus (Words You Never Thought)
Demonic	More Words
Demonically	More Words
Demonstrable	Top 50
Demonstrably	Top 50
Demure	Bonus (Fancy Words)
Demurred	Bonus (Fancy Words)
Demurring	Bonus (Fancy Words)
Demurringly	Bonus (Fancy Words)

Deplorable	More Words
Deplorably	More Words
Depravedly	Bonus (Adverbs Whose Company)
Destroyed	More Words
Detestably	Bonus (Adverbs Whose Company)
Devilish	More Words
Devilishly	More Words
Deviously	Bonus (Adverbs Whose Company)
Dexterously	Bonus (Adverbs Whose Company)
Dialogue	More Words
Did not bother	More Words
Didactic	Bonus (Fancy Words)
Didactically	Bonus (Fancy Words)
Diffident	Bonus (Fancy Words)
Diffidently	Bonus (Fancy Words)
Dim	Bonus (Words You Never Thought)
Dimly	Bonus (Words You Never Thought)
Dimwitted	Bonus (Words You Never Thought)
Dimwittedly	Bonus (Words You Never Thought)
Directly	More Words
Disconcertedly	Bonus (Adverbs Whose Company)
Disconcertingly	Bonus (Adverbs Whose Company)
Discretionarily	Bonus (Adverbs Whose Company)
Discretionary	Bonus (Lawyerly Words)
Discriminating	More Words

Discriminatingly	More Words
Disdainful	More Words
Disdainfully	More Words
Disingenuous	More Words
Disingenuously	More Words
Disjointed	More Words
Disjointedly	More Words
Disjunctive	Bonus (Words To Give Your Writing)
Disjunctively	Bonus (Words To Give Your Writing)
Disparaging	More Words
Disparagingly	More Words
Disposable	More Words
Disposably	More Words
Dispositive	More Words
Dispositively	More Words
Disputatious	Bonus (Fancy Words)
Disputatiously	Bonus (Fancy Words)
Dissembling	Bonus (Fancy Words)
Dissemblingly	Bonus (Fancy Words)
Disturbed	More Words
Disturbing	More Words
Disturbingly	More Words
Do not bother	More Words
Dodgy	More Words
Don't disagree	More Words

Doubtful	More Words
Doubtfully	More Words
Downright	More Words
Downrightly	More Words
Drab	More Words
Drably	More Words
Dreadful	More Words
Dreadfully	More Words
Drearily	More Words
Dreary	More Words
Droll	More Words
Drolly	More Words
Dubious	More Words
Dubiously	More Words
Dull	More Words
Dully	More Words
Dumb	More Words
Dumbfounded	More Words
Dumbfoundedly	More Words
Dumbly	More Words
Duplicative	Bonus (Words To Give Your Writing)
Duplicitous	More Words
Duplicitously	More Words
Easily	More Words
Easy	More Words

Eclectic	Bonus (Fancy Words)
Eclectically	Bonus (Fancy Words)
Economically	Bonus (Adverbs Whose Company)
Ecumenical	Bonus (Fancy Words)
Ecumenically	Bonus (Fancy Words)
Edifying	Bonus (Fancy Words)
Edifyingly	Bonus (Fancy Words)
Effervescent	Bonus (Fancy Words)
Effervescently	Bonus (Fancy Words)
Effusive	Bonus (Fancy Words)
Effusively	Bonus (Fancy Words)
Egomaniacal	Bonus (Go-To Choices)
Egomaniacally	Bonus (Go-To Choices)
Egotistical	Bonus (Words You Never Thought)
Egotistically	Bonus (Words You Never Thought)
Egregious	Top 50
Egregiously	Top 50
Elucidating	Bonus (Fancy Words)
Embarrassedly	Bonus (Adverbs Whose Company)
Embarrassingly	Bonus (Adverbs Whose Company)
Emphatic	More Words
Emphatically	More Words
Emptily	Bonus (Adverbs Whose Company)
Endemic	More Words
Endemically	More Words

Endless	More Words
Endlessly	More Words
Enervated	Bonus (Fancy Words)
Enervating	Bonus (Fancy Words)
Enigmatic	More Words
Enigmatically	More Words
Enlighteningly	Bonus (Adverbs Whose Company)
Enormous	More Words
Enormously	More Words
Entire	More Words
Entirely	More Words
Ephemeral	Bonus (Fancy Words)
Ephemerally	Bonus (Fancy Words)
Epitomic	Bonus (Fancy Words)
Epitomical	Bonus (Fancy Words)
Erroneous	More Words
Erroneously	More Words
Esoteric	Bonus (Fancy Words)
Esoterically	Bonus (Fancy Words)
Especial	More Words
Especially	More Words
Essential	More Words
Essentially	More Words
Euphemistic	Bonus (Fancy Words)
Euphemistically	Bonus (Fancy Words)

Eventful	More Words
Eventfully	More Words
Evermore	More Words
Evident	More Words
Evidently	More Words, Bonus (Sentence Adverbs)
Evilly	Bonus (Adverbs Whose Company)
Eviscerated	More Words
Eviscerating	More Words
Exact	More Words
Exactly	More Words
Exaggeratedly	Bonus (Adverbs Whose Company)
Exaltedly	Bonus (Adverbs Whose Company)
Exasperated	More Words
Exasperatedly	More Words
Exasperating	More Words
Exasperatingly	More Words
Exceeding	More Words
Exceedingly	More Words
Excellently	Bonus (Adverbs Whose Company)
Excessive	Top 50
Excessively	Top 50
Exclamation marks	More Words
Excruciating	More Words
Excruciatingly	More Words
Exemplarily	More Words

Expansive	More Words
Expansively	More Words
Explosive	More Words
Explosively	More Words
Exponential	More Words
Exponentially	More Words
Extraneous	More Words
Extraneously	More Words
Extreme	More Words
Extremely	More Words
Exuberant	Bonus (Fancy Words)
Exuberantly	Bonus (Fancy Words)
Exultant	Bonus (Fancy Words)
Exulting	Bonus (Fancy Words)
Exultingly	Bonus (Fancy Words)
Fabled	Bonus (Words You Never Thought)
Fabulous	Bonus (Words You Never Thought)
Fabulously	Bonus (Words You Never Thought)
Facetious	Bonus (Fancy Words)
Facetiously	Bonus (Fancy Words)
Facial	More Words
Facially	More Words
Facilitative	More Words
Facilitatively	More Words
Fact-barren	More Words

Failed	More Words
Failing	More Words
Failingly	More Words
Faintly	More Words
Fake	More Words
Fallacious	More Words
Fallaciously	More Words
False	Top 50
Falsely	Top 50
Familiarly	Bonus (Adverbs Whose Company)
Fanciful	More Words
Fancifully	Bonus (Adverbs Whose Company)
Fancifully	More Words
Fancily	Bonus (Adverbs Whose Company)
Farcical	More Words
Farcically	More Words
Fatal	More Words
Fatally	More Words
Fatuous	Bonus (Fancy Words)
Fatuously	Bonus (Fancy Words)
Feckless	Bonus (Fancy Words)
Fecklessly	Bonus (Fancy Words)
Felicitous	Bonus (Fancy Words)
Felicitously	Bonus (Fancy Words)
Figurative	More Words

Figuratively	More Words
Filthily	Bonus (Adverbs Whose Company)
Finally	More Words
Fishily	Bonus (Adverbs Whose Company)
Fishing	More Words
Fishy	Bonus (Words You Never Thought)
Flagrant	More Words
Flagrantly	More Words
Flailing	Bonus (Words You Never Thought)
Flakily	Bonus (Adverbs Whose Company)
Flaky	Bonus (Words You Never Thought)
Flatly	More Words
Flightily	Bonus (Adverbs Whose Company)
Flighty	Bonus (Words You Never Thought)
Flintily	Bonus (Adverbs Whose Company)
Flinty	Bonus (Words You Never Thought)
Flippant	More Words
Flippantly	More Words
Flummoxed	Bonus (Fancy Words)
Foolish	More Words
Foolishly	More Words
Formalistic	Bonus (Go-To Choices)
Formalistically	Bonus (Go-To Choices)
Formulaic	Bonus (Words To Give Your Writing)
Formulaically	Bonus (Words To Give Your Writing)

Fortuitous	More Words
Fortuitously	More Words
Frank	More Words
Frankly	More Words, Bonus (Sentence Adverbs)
Fraudulent	Top 50
Fraudulently	Top 50
Fraught	Bonus (Fancy Words)
Freakily	Bonus (Adverbs Whose Company)
Freaky	Bonus (Words You Never Thought)
Freighted	Bonus (Fancy Words)
Frighteningly	Bonus (Adverbs Whose Company)
Frivolous	Top 50
Frivolously	Top 50
Frustrated	More Words
Frustratedly	More Words
Frustrating	More Words
Frustratingly	More Words
Fully	More Words
Fulsome	More Words
Fulsomely	More Words
Fundamental	More Words
Fundamentally	More Words
Funkily	Bonus (Adverbs Whose Company)
Funky	Bonus (Words You Never Thought)
Funnily	More Words

Futile	More Words
Futilely	More Words
Galactic	More Words
Galactically	More Words
Gamesmanship	More Words
Garbled	More Words
Garden-variety	More Words
Gargantuan	More Words
Gargantuanly	More Words
Garish	Bonus (Fancy Words)
Garishly	Bonus (Fancy Words)
Garrulous	Bonus (Fancy Words)
Garrulously	Bonus (Fancy Words)
Gauche	Bonus (Fancy Words)
Gauchely	Bonus (Fancy Words)
Gaudily	Bonus (Adverbs Whose Company)
Gaudy	Bonus (Fancy Words)
General	Top 50
Generalized	More Words
Generally	Top 50
Genial	Bonus (Fancy Words)
Genially	Bonus (Fancy Words)
Genteel	Bonus (Fancy Words)
Genteelly	Bonus (Fancy Words)
Genuine	Top 50

Genuinely	Top 50
Germane	Bonus (Fancy Words)
Germanely	Bonus (Fancy Words)
Ghoulish	Bonus (Words You Never Thought)
Ghoulishly	Bonus (Words You Never Thought)
Gigantic	More Words
Gigantically	More Words
Ginormous	More Words
Glaring	More Words
Glaringly	More Words
Glib	More Words
Glibly	More Words
Gnarled	More Words
Gnarly	More Words
Gnawing	Bonus (Words You Never Thought)
Gnawingly	Bonus (Words You Never Thought)
Good	More Words
Goodly	More Words
Goofily	More Words
Goofy	More Words
Graceless	More Words
Gracelessly	More Words
Gracious	More Words
Graciously	More Words
Grandiose	More Words

Grandiosely	More Words
Granular	More Words
Granularized	More Words
Granularly	More Words
Gratuitous	More Words
Gratuitously	More Words
Grave	More Words
Gravely	More Words
Great	More Words
Greatly	More Words
Grisly	More Words
Grizzled	More Words
Groovily	More Words
Groovy	More Words
Gross	Top 50
Grossly	Top 50
Grouchily	Bonus (Adverbs Whose Company)
Groundbreaking	More Words
Groundbreakingly	More Words
Groundless	Top 50
Groundlessly	Top 50
Grudging	More Words
Grudgingly	More Words
Gruesome	More Words
Gruesomely	More Words

Grungily	Bonus (Words You Never Thought)
Grungy	Bonus (Words You Never Thought)
Guiltily	Bonus (Adverbs Whose Company)
Hackneyed	More Words
Halfhearted	More Words
Halfheartedly	More Words
Hallowed	Bonus (Fancy Words)
Happily	More Words
Happy	More Words
Hardly	More Words
Hastily	More Words
Hasty	More Words
Haughtily	Bonus (Adverbs Whose Company)
Haughty	Bonus (Fancy Words)
Headily	Bonus (Adverbs Whose Company)
Helpful	More Words
Helpfully	More Words
Highfalutin	More Words
Highly	More Words
Historic	More Words
Historical	More Words
Historically	More Words
Honest	More Words
Honestly	More Words, Bonus (Sentence Adverbs)
Hoodwinked	Bonus (Words You Never Thought)

Hopeful	More Words
Hopefully	More Words, Bonus (Sentence Adverbs)
Horrific	More Words
Horrifically	More Words
Hot-blooded	More Words
Hubristic	Bonus (Fancy Words)
Hubristically	Bonus (Fancy Words)
Huge	More Words
Hugely	More Words
Humble	More Words
Humbly	More Words
Hyperbolic	More Words
Hyperbolically	More Words
Hypocritical	More Words
Hypocritically	More Words
Hypothetically	Bonus (Sentence Adverbs)
Hysterical	Bonus (Words You Never Thought)
Hysterically	Bonus (Words You Never Thought)
Ideally	Bonus (Sentence Adverbs)
Idiotic	More Words
Idiotically	More Words
Ignoble	More Words
Ignobly	More Words
Ignominious	More Words
Ignominiously	More Words

Ignorant	More Words
Ignorantly	More Words
Ill-advised	More Words
Ill-advisedly	More Words
Ill-informed	More Words
Ill-informedly	More Words
Illegitimate	More Words
Illegitimately	More Words
Illogical	More Words
Illogically	More Words
Illusorily	Bonus (Adverbs Whose Company)
Illusory	Bonus (Fancy Words)
Imaginarily	Bonus (Adverbs Whose Company)
Immediate	More Words
Immediately	More Words
Immense	More Words
Immensely	More Words
Imminent	More Words
Imminently	More Words
Immutable	More Words
Immutably	More Words
Impending	More Words
Impenetrable	More Words
Impenetrably	More Words
Imperative	More Words

Imperatively	More Words
Imperfect	More Words
Imperfectly	More Words
Impertinent	Bonus (Fancy Words)
Impertinently	Bonus (Adverbs Whose Company)
Implacable	More Words
Implacably	More Words
Impossible	More Words
Impossibly	More Words
Impotent	Bonus (Words You Never Thought)
Impotently	Bonus (Words You Never Thought)
Impressive	More Words
Impressively	More Words
Impudent	More Words
Impudently	More Words
In all honesty	More Words
Inaccurate	More Words
Inaccurately	More Words
Inadvertent	More Words
Inadvertently	More Words
Inartful	More Words
Inartfully	More Words
Inauspicious	More Words
Inauspiciously	More Words
Incalculable	More Words

Incalculably	More Words
Incessant	More Words
Incessantly	More Words
Inchoate	More Words
Inchoately	More Words
Incidental	More Words
Incidentally	More Words, Bonus (Sentence Adverbs)
Incipient	More Words
Incipiently	More Words
Incoherent	More Words
Incoherently	More Words
Incompetent	More Words
Incompetently	More Words
Inconceivable	More Words
Inconceivably	More Words
Inconclusive	More Words
Inconclusively	More Words
Incongruent	More Words
Incongruently	More Words
Inconsequential	More Words
Inconsequentially	More Words
Inconspicuous	More Words
Inconspicuously	More Words
Incontrovertible	More Words
Incontrovertibly	More Words

Incorrect	More Words
Incorrectly	More Words
Incorrigible	More Words
Incorrigibly	More Words
Increasing	More Words
Increasingly	More Words
Incredible	Top 50
Incredibly	Top 50
Incredulously	Bonus (Adverbs Whose Company)
Indeed	Top 50
Indefinite	More Words
Indefinitely	More Words
Indescribable	More Words
Indescribably	More Words
Indestructibly	Bonus (Adverbs Whose Company)
Indeterminate	More Words
Indeterminately	More Words
Indisputable	Top 50
Indisputably	Top 50
Indubitable	More Words
Indubitably	More Words
Inept	More Words
Ineptly	More Words
Inevitable	More Words
Inevitably	More Words

Inexcusable	More Words
Inexcusably	More Words
Inexorable	More Words
Inexorably	More Words
Infamous	More Words
Infamously	More Words
Infernal	Bonus (Words You Never Thought)
Infernally	Bonus (Words You Never Thought)
Infinite	More Words
Infinitely	More Words
Inflated	More Words
Inherent	More Words
Inherently	More Words
Inimical	More Words
Inimically	More Words
Innumerable	More Words
Innumerably	More Words
Inobstrusive	More Words
Inobstrusively	More Words
Inscrutable	More Words
Inscrutably	More Words
Insignificant	More Words
Insignificantly	More Words
Insipid	More Words
Insipidly	More Words

Instant	More Words
Insubstantial	More Words
Insubstantially	More Words
Insulting	More Words
Intentional	More Words
Intentionally	More Words
Interesting	More Words
Interestingly	More Words, Bonus (Sentence Adverbs)
Interlocutory	Bonus (Lawyerly Words)
Interminable	More Words
Interminably	More Words
Intermittent	More Words
Intermittently	More Words
Intolerable	More Words
Intolerably	More Words
Intractable	More Words
Intractably	More Words
Invalidated	Bonus (Lawyerly Words)
Invalidating	Bonus (Lawyerly Words)
Involuntarily	Bonus (Lawyerly Words)
Involuntary	Bonus (Lawyerly Words)
Irksome	More Words
Irksomely	More Words
Ironic	More Words
Ironical	More Words

Ironically	More Words, Bonus (Sentence Adverbs)
Irony	More Words
Irresistible	More Words
Irresistibly	More Words
Irrespective	More Words
Irrespectively	More Words
Irreverently	Bonus (Adverbs Whose Company)
Irritating	More Words
Irritatingly	More Words
Is it any wonder	More Words
It is important to note	More Words
It is little wonder	More Words
It is no wonder	More Words
Janky	Bonus (Words You Never Thought)
Judgmental	More Words
Judgmentally	More Words
Judgy	More Words
Juicy	Bonus (Words You Never Thought)
Jury-rigged	More Words
Just	More Words
Justly	More Words
Keen	More Words
Keenly	More Words
Kind	More Words
Kindly	More Words

Kitschy	Bonus (Words You Never Thought)
Knowing	More Words
Knowingly	More Words
Lamentable	More Words
Lamentably	More Words
Lamented	More Words
Lamentedly	More Words
Large	More Words
Largely	More Words
Lascivious	Bonus (Lawyerly Words)
Lasciviously	Bonus (Lawyerly Words)
Laudable	More Words
Laudably	More Words
Laudatorily	Bonus (Adverbs Whose Company)
Laudatorily	More Words
Laudatory	Bonus (Fancy Words)
Laudatory	More Words
Legalistic	Bonus (Lawyerly Words)
Legalistically	Bonus (Lawyerly Words)
Legitimate	More Words
Legitimately	More Words
Lewd	Bonus (Lawyerly Words)
Lewdly	Bonus (Lawyerly Words)
Liberal	More Words
Liberally	More Words

Licentious	Bonus (Lawyerly Words)
Licentiously	Bonus (Lawyerly Words)
Lightly	More Words
Likely	More Words
Limited	More Words
Limitedly	More Words
Limitless	More Words
Literal	Top 50
Literally	Top 50
Litigious	Bonus (Lawyerly Words)
Litigiously	Bonus (Lawyerly Words)
Limitlessly	More Words
Loathsome	More Words
Loathsomely	More Words
Loony	Bonus (Words You Never Thought)
Loopy	Bonus (Words You Never Thought)
Loose	More Words
Loosely	More Words
Loquacious	More Words
Loquaciously	More Words
Magical	More Words
Magically	More Words
Manifest	More Words
Manifestly	More Words
Many	Top 50

Marginal	More Words
Marginally	More Words
Massive	More Words
Massively	More Words
Material	More Words
Materially	More Words
Meaningless	More Words
Meaninglessly	More Words
Measly	More Words
Mendacious	Bonus (Fancy Words)
Mendaciously	Bonus (Fancy Words)
Mere	Top 50
Merely	Top 50
Meritless	Top 50
Meritlessly	Top 50
Miraculous	More Words
Miraculously	More Words
Misbegotten	Bonus (Fancy Words)
Mistaken	Top 50
Mistakenly	Top 50
Momentous	More Words
Momentously	More Words
Most likely because	More Words
Multilateral	Bonus (Words To Give Your Writing)
Multilaterally	Bonus (Words To Give Your Writing)

Multiplicitous	Bonus (Lawyerly Words)
Multiplicitously	Bonus (Lawyerly Words)
Mundane	More Words
Mundanely	More Words
Murkily	Bonus (Adverbs Whose Company)
Myopic	Bonus (Fancy Words)
Myopically	Bonus (Fancy Words)
Mysterious	More Words
Mysteriously	More Words
Naive	More Words
Naively	More Words
Naked	Bonus (Words You Never Thought)
Nakedly	Bonus (Words You Never Thought)
Narrow	More Words
Narrowly	More Words
Nastily	Bonus (Adverbs Whose Company)
Naturally	Bonus (Sentence Adverbs)
Nearly	More Words
Necessarily	Top 50
Necessary	Top 50
Needless	Top 50
Needlessly	Top 50
Nefarious	Bonus (Fancy Words)
Nefariously	Bonus (Fancy Words)
Negated	Bonus (Lawyerly Words)

Negating	Bonus (Lawyerly Words)
Negligent	Bonus (Lawyerly Words)
Negligently	Bonus (Lawyerly Words)
Negligible	More Words
Negligibly	More Words
Nervily	Bonus (Adverbs Whose Company)
Never	Top 50
Never-ending	More Words
Never-endingly	More Words
Nihilistic	Bonus (Fancy Words)
Nihilistically	Bonus (Fancy Words)
Noble	More Words
Nobly	More Words
Noisily	More Words
Noisy	More Words
Nonessential	More Words
Nonessentially	More Words
Nonexistent	More Words
Nonplussed	More Words
Nonsensical	More Words
Nonsensically	More Words
Notable	More Words
Notably	More Words
Noteworthily	More Words
Noteworthy	More Words

Nugatory	Bonus (Fancy Words)
Nullified	More Words
Nullifying	More Words
Numbly	Bonus (Adverbs Whose Company)
Numerous	More Words
Obedient	More Words
Obediently	More Words
Obeisant	More Words
Obeisantly	More Words
Obfuscated	More Words
Obfuscating	More Words
Oblique	More Words
Obliquely	More Words
Obliterated	More Words
Obnoxious	More Words
Obnoxiously	More Words
Obscene	More Words
Obscenely	More Words
Obsequious	More Words
Obsequiously	More Words
Obsolescent	More Words
Obsolescently	More Words
Obsolete	More Words
Obsoletely	More Words
Obstinate	More Words

Obstinately	More Words
Obtrusive	More Words
Obtrusively	More Words
Obtuse	More Words
Obtusely	More Words
Obviated	More Words
Obviating	More Words
Obvious	Top 50
Obviously	Top 50
Odious	Bonus (Fancy Words)
Odiously	Bonus (Fancy Words)
Off-putting	More Words
Omnifarious	More Words
Omnipotent	Bonus (Fancy Words)
Omnipotently	Bonus (Fancy Words)
Omnipresent	Bonus (Fancy Words)
Omniscient	Bonus (Fancy Words)
Omnisciently	Bonus (Fancy Words)
On its face	More Words
Onerous	More Words
Onerously	More Words
Ontological	Bonus (Fancy Words)
Ontologically	Bonus (Fancy Words)
Operational	Bonus (Words To Give Your Writing)
Operationally	Bonus (Words To Give Your Writing)

Operative	Bonus (Words To Give Your Writing)
Operatively	Bonus (Words To Give Your Writing)
Oppositional	Bonus (Words To Give Your Writing)
Oppositionally	Bonus (Words To Give Your Writing)
Optionally	Bonus (Adverbs Whose Company)
Ornery	Bonus (Words You Never Thought)
Ostensible	Top 50
Ostensibly	Top 50
Ostentatious	More Words
Ostentatiously	More Words
Outraged	More Words
Outrageous	More Words
Outrageously	More Words
Overblown	More Words
Overheated	More Words
Overheatedly	More Words
Overlappingly	Bonus (Adverbs Whose Company)
Overly	More Words
Overrated	More Words
Overt	More Words
Overtly	More Words
Overweening	Bonus (Fancy Words)
Overweeningly	Bonus (Adverbs Whose Company)
Overwrought	Bonus (Fancy Words)
Oxymoronic	More Words

Oxymoronically	More Words
Paradigmatic	More Words
Paradigmatically	More Words
Paradoxical	More Words
Paradoxically	More Words
Parasitic	Bonus (Words You Never Thought)
Parasitically	Bonus (Words You Never Thought)
Parenthetical	More Words
Parenthetically	More Words
Parochial	Bonus (Fancy Words)
Parochially	Bonus (Fancy Words)
Partial	More Words
Partially	More Words
Particularly	Top 50
Partly	More Words
Patently	More Words
Pathetic	More Words
Pathetically	More Words
Patronizing	More Words
Patronizingly	More Words
Peculiar	More Words
Peculiarly	More Words
Pecuniarily	Bonus (Fancy Words)
Pecuniary	Bonus (Fancy Words)
Pedantic	More Words

Pedantically	More Words
Peevish	Bonus (Words You Never Thought)
Peevishly	Bonus (Words You Never Thought)
Pejorative	More Words
Pejoratively	More Words
Pellucid	More Words
Pellucidly	More Words
Pensive	Bonus (Fancy Words)
Pensively	Bonus (Fancy Words)
Penultimate	More Words
Penultimately	More Words
Perceptibly	Bonus (Adverbs Whose Company)
Perennial	More Words
Perennially	More Words
Perfectly	More Words
Perfunctorily	More Words
Perfunctory	More Words
Perjured	Bonus (Lawyerly Words)
Perjurious	Bonus (Lawyerly Words)
Perjuriously	Bonus (Lawyerly Words)
Perpetual	More Words
Perpetually	More Words
Perplexed	More Words
Perplexedly	More Words
Perplexing	More Words

Perplexingly	More Words
Persistent	More Words
Persistently	More Words
Persnickety	Bonus (Words You Never Thought)
Perturbed	Bonus (Fancy Words)
Perturbing	Bonus (Fancy Words)
Perturbingly	Bonus (Fancy Words)
Peskily	Bonus (Adverbs Whose Company)
Pesky	Bonus (Words You Never Thought)
Pesty	Bonus (Words You Never Thought)
Pettily	Bonus (Adverbs Whose Company)
Petty	Bonus (Words You Never Thought)
Petulant	Bonus (Fancy Words)
Petulantly	Bonus (Fancy Words)
Philistine	More Words
Phonily	Bonus (Adverbs Whose Company)
Phony	Bonus (Words You Never Thought)
Pigheaded	More Words
Pigheadedly	More Words
Piquant	Bonus (Fancy Words)
Piquantly	Bonus (Fancy Words)
Plain	Top 50
Plainly	Top 50
Pleasant	More Words
Pleasantly	More Words

Plethora	More Words
Poached	More Words
Pointless	More Words
Pointlessly	More Words
Polemic	Bonus (Fancy Words)
Polemically	Bonus (Fancy Words)
Possible	More Words
Possibly	More Words
Post hoc	More Words
Potential	More Words
Potentially	More Words
Precedential	Bonus (Lawyerly Words)
Precedentially	Bonus (Lawyerly Words)
Precedingly	Bonus (Adverbs Whose Company)
Precious	More Words
Preciously	More Words
Precipitous	More Words
Precipitously	More Words
Precise	More Words
Precisely	More Words
Preclusive	Bonus (Lawyerly Words)
Preclusively	Bonus (Lawyerly Words)
Precursory	Bonus (Fancy Words)
Predictable	More Words
Predictably	More Words, Bonus (Sentence Adverbs)

Preeminent	More Words
Preeminently	More Words
Prefatorily	More Words
Prefatory	More Words
Preposterous	More Words
Preposterously	More Words
Presumable	More Words
Presumably	More Words, Bonus (Sentence Adverbs)
Presumptive	More Words
Presumptively	More Words
Presumptuous	More Words
Presumptuously	More Words
Prettily	Bonus (Adverbs Whose Company)
Prevalent	Bonus (Fancy Words)
Prevalently	Bonus (Adverbs Whose Company)
Prime	More Words
Primitive	More Words
Primitively	More Words
Primordial	Bonus (Fancy Words)
Primordially	Bonus (Fancy Words)
Prior to	More Words
Probative	More Words
Probatively	More Words
Problematic	More Words
Problematically	More Words

Profane	More Words
Profanely	More Words
Profanity	More Words
Profound	More Words
Profoundly	More Words
Proletarian	Bonus (Fancy Words)
Prolix	More Words
Prolixly	More Words
Prompt	More Words
Promptly	More Words
Proper	More Words
Properly	More Words
Prophetic	More Words
Prophetical	More Words
Prophetically	More Words
Prophylactic	More Words
Prophylactically	More Words
Propinquitous	Bonus (Fancy Words)
Propitious	More Words
Propitiously	More Words
Prosperously	Bonus (Adverbs Whose Company)
Proverbial	More Words
Proverbially	More Words
Provincial	Bonus (Fancy Words)
Provincially	Bonus (Fancy Words)

Provocative	More Words
Provocatively	More Words
Pugnacious	Bonus (Fancy Words)
Pugnaciously	Bonus (Fancy Words)
Punchily	Bonus (Adverbs Whose Company)
Punchy	Bonus (Words You Never Thought)
Punily	Bonus (Adverbs Whose Company)
Puny	Bonus (Words You Never Thought)
Purported	More Words
Purportedly	More Words
Purposeful	More Words
Purposefully	More Words
Purposely	More Words
Purposive	Bonus (Fancy Words)
Purposively	Bonus (Fancy Words)
Pursuant to	More Words
Putrid	More Words
Putridly	More Words
Quaint	More Words
Quaintly	More Words
Qualified	More Words
Qualifiedly	More Words
Qualitative	Bonus (Words To Give Your Writing)
Qualitatively	Bonus (Words To Give Your Writing)
Quality	More Words

Quantitative	Bonus (Words To Give Your Writing)
Quantitatively	Bonus (Words To Give Your Writing)
Quashed	Bonus (Lawyerly Words)
Questionable	More Words
Questionably	More Words
Quintessential	More Words
Quintessentially	More Words
Quirkily	Bonus (Adverbs Whose Company)
Quirky	Bonus (Words You Never Thought)
Quixotic	More Words
Quixotically	More Words
Quizzical	Bonus (Fancy Words)
Quizzically	Bonus (Adverbs Whose Company)
Quotidian	More Words
Radical	More Words
Radically	More Words
Random	More Words
Randomly	More Words
Rare	More Words
Rarely	More Words
Rather	Top 50
Reactionarily	Bonus (Go-To Choices)
Reactionary	Bonus (Go-To Choices)
Readily	Top 50
Really	Top 50

Reasonable	More Words
Reasonably	More Words
Recapitulated	Bonus (Go-To Choices)
Reciprocal	Bonus (Lawyerly Words)
Reciprocally	Bonus (Lawyerly Words)
Recursive	Bonus (Fancy Words)
Recursively	Bonus (Fancy Words)
Redoubtable	Bonus (Fancy Words)
Redoubtably	Bonus (Fancy Words)
Reductive	Bonus (Fancy Words)
Reductively	Bonus (Fancy Words)
Regrettable	More Words
Regrettably	More Words, Bonus (Sentence Adverbs)
Reiterative	Bonus (Words To Give Your Writing)
Reiteratively	Bonus (Words To Give Your Writing)
Relative	More Words
Relatively	More Words
Reluctant	More Words
Reluctantly	More Words
Remarkable	Top 50
Remarkably	Top 50, Bonus (Sentence Adverbs)
Remote	More Words
Remotely	More Words
Repeated	More Words
Repeatedly	More Words

Repentant	More Words
Repentantly	More Words
Repetitive	More Words
Repetitively	More Words
Reproachful	Bonus (Fancy Words)
Reproachfully	Bonus (Fancy Words)
Repudiated	More Words
Repudiating	More Words
Repugnant	More Words
Repugnantly	More Words
Reservedly	Bonus (Adverbs Whose Company)
Resounding	More Words
Resoundingly	More Words
Respect	More Words
Respectful	More Words
Respectfully	More Words
Restrainedly	Bonus (Adverbs Whose Company)
Resultingly	Bonus (Adverbs Whose Company)
Retaliatorily	More Words
Retaliatory	More Words
Revolutionarily	Bonus (Adverbs Whose Company)
Rhetorical questions	More Words
Ridiculous	More Words
Ridiculously	More Words
Risible	Bonus (Fancy Words)

Risibly	Bonus (Fancy Words)
Rockily	Bonus (Fancy Words)
Rough	More Words
Roughly	More Words
Routine	More Words
Routinely	More Words
Rude	More Words
Rudely	More Words
Rueful	Bonus (Fancy Words)
Ruefully	Bonus (Fancy Words)
Running	Bonus (Words You Never Thought)
Sacred	More Words
Sacredly	More Words
Sacrificially	Bonus (Adverbs Whose Company)
Sacrosanct	More Words
Sadly	More Words
Sagacious	More Words
Sagaciously	More Words
Sage	More Words
Sagely	More Words
Salient	More Words
Saliently	More Words
Sanctimonious	More Words
Sanctimoniously	More Words
Sanguine	More Words

Sanguinely	More Words
Sardonic	Bonus (Fancy Words)
Sardonically	Bonus (Fancy Words)
Saucily	More Words
Saucy	More Words
Savage	Bonus (Words You Never Thought)
Savagely	Bonus (Words You Never Thought)
Scarce	More Words
Scarcely	More Words
Scarily	Bonus (Adverbs Whose Company)
Scoundrelly	Bonus (Adverbs Whose Company)
Scrawny	Bonus (Words You Never Thought)
Screechy	Bonus (Words You Never Thought)
Seeming	Top 50
Seemingly	Top 50
Seldom	More Words
Self-evident	More Words
Self-evidently	More Words
Self-explanatorily	More Words
Self-explanatory	More Words
Selfish	More Words
Selfishly	More Words
Self-serving	More Words
Semantic	More Words
Semantically	More Words

Senseless	More Words
Senselessly	More Words
Sensible	More Words
Sensibly	More Words
Serious	Top 50
Seriously	Top 50
Severe	More Words
Severely	More Words
Shakily	More Words
Shaky	More Words
Shameless	More Words
Shamelessly	More Words
Sharp	More Words
Sharply	More Words
Shining	More Words
Shocking	More Words
Shockingly	More Words
Short	More Words
Shortly	More Words
Shortsighted	More Words
Shortsightedly	More Words
Shrewd	More Words
Shrewdly	More Words
Shrewish	Bonus (Words You Never Thought)
Shrill	Bonus (Words You Never Thought)

Shrilly	Bonus (Words You Never Thought)
Sickening	More Words
Sickeningly	More Words
Significant	More Words
Significantly	More Words
Similarly	Bonus (Sentence Adverbs)
Simple	More Words
Simplified	More Words
Simplifying	More Words
Simplistic	More Words
Simply	Top 50
Singular	More Words
Singularly	More Words
Situational	Bonus (Words To Give Your Writing)
Situationally	Bonus (Words To Give Your Writing)
Skeptical	More Words
Skeptically	More Words
Slavish	More Words
Slavishly	More Words
Slight	More Words
Slightly	More Words
Sloppily	More Words
Sloppy	More Words
Slovenly	Bonus (Words You Never Thought)
Smarmily	Bonus (Adverbs Whose Company)

Smarmy	Bonus (Words You Never Thought)
Smooth	More Words
Smoothly	More Words
Smugly	Bonus (Adverbs Whose Company)
Sneakily	Bonus (Adverbs Whose Company)
Sneaky	Bonus (Words You Never Thought)
Solemn	More Words
Solemnly	More Words
Solicitous	Bonus (Fancy Words)
Solicitously	Bonus (Fancy Words)
Sophistic	Bonus (Fancy Words)
Sophistically	Bonus (Fancy Words)
Sophisticatedly	Bonus (Adverbs Whose Company)
Sparing	More Words
Sparingly	More Words
Speaks for itself	More Words
Specifically	Bonus (Sentence Adverbs)
Spectacular	More Words
Spectacularly	More Words
Speculatively	Bonus (Adverbs Whose Company)
Speechless	Bonus (Words You Never Thought)
Speechlessly	Bonus (Adverbs Whose Company)
Speedily	Bonus (Adverbs Whose Company)
Spiritedly	Bonus (Adverbs Whose Company)
Spoiled	Bonus (Words You Never Thought)

Sporadic	Bonus (Fancy Words)
Sporadically	Bonus (Fancy Words)
Sporting	More Words
Sportingly	More Words
Square	More Words
Squarely	More Words
Stably	Bonus (Adverbs Whose Company)
Standardly	Bonus (Adverbs Whose Company)
Startlingly	Bonus (Adverbs Whose Company)
Stealthily	Bonus (Adverbs Whose Company)
Steeply	Bonus (Adverbs Whose Company)
Stern	More Words
Sternly	More Words
Stickily	More Words
Sticky	More Words
Stipulated	Bonus (Lawyerly Words)
Stonily	Bonus (Adverbs Whose Company)
Stoutly	Bonus (Adverbs Whose Company)
Straightforward	More Words
Straightforwardly	More Words
Straightly	Bonus (Adverbs Whose Company)
Strange	More Words
Strangely	More Words, Bonus (Sentence Adverbs)
Strict	More Words
Strictly	More Words

Strike at the very core of	More Words
Strong	More Words
Strongly	More Words
Studious	More Words
Studiously	More Words
Stupefied	More Words
Stupefying	More Words
Stupendous	More Words
Stupendously	More Words
Stupid	More Words
Stupidly	More Words
Subjugated	Bonus (Fancy Words)
Subjugating	Bonus (Fancy Words)
Subsequent	More Words
Subsequently	More Words
Substantial	More Words
Substantially	More Words
Succinct	More Words
Succinctly	More Words
Sudden	More Words
Suddenly	More Words
Sullied	More Words
Super	More Words
Supercilious	Bonus (Fancy Words)
Superciliously	Bonus (Fancy Words)

Supposed	Top 50
Supposedly	Top 50
Sure	More Words
Surely	More Words
Surprisingly	Bonus (Sentence Adverbs)
Suspicious	More Words
Suspiciously	More Words
Sweeping	More Words
Sweepingly	More Words
Swift	More Words
Swiftly	More Words
Swimmingly	Bonus (Words You Never Thought)
Symbiotic	Bonus (Fancy Words)
Symbiotically	Bonus (Fancy Words)
Symbolic	More Words
Symbolically	More Words
Tackily	Bonus (Adverbs Whose Company)
Tacky	Bonus (Words You Never Thought)
Tamely	Bonus (Adverbs Whose Company)
Tastily	Bonus (Adverbs Whose Company)
Tautological	Bonus (Fancy Words)
Tautologically	Bonus (Fancy Words)
Technical	More Words
Technically	More Words, Bonus (Sentence Adverbs)
Tedious	More Words

Tediously	More Words
Teleological	Bonus (Fancy Words)
Teleologically	Bonus (Fancy Words)
Telling	More Words
Tellingly	More Words
Tenable	More Words
Tenably	More Words
Terrible	More Words
Terribly	More Words
Terrific	More Words
Terrifically	More Words
Thankfully	Bonus (Sentence Adverbs)
Thankless	More Words
Thanklessly	More Words
The truth is	More Words
Theoretical	More Words
Theoretically	More Words, Bonus (Sentence Adverbs)
Thin	More Words
Thinly	More Words
Thornily	More Words
Thorny	More Words
Thorough	More Words
Thoroughly	More Words
Thoughtless	More Words
Thoughtlessly	More Words

Tickled	Bonus (Words You Never Thought)
Timid	More Words
Timidly	More Words
Tiny	Bonus (Words You Never Thought)
Tired	More Words
Tiresome	More Words
Tiresomely	More Words
Tiringly	Bonus (Adverbs Whose Company)
Tolerable	More Words
Tolerably	More Words
Too clever by half	More Words
Too cute by half	More Words
Tortious	Bonus (Lawyerly Words)
Tortiously	Bonus (Lawyerly Words)
Tortured	More Words
Total	Top 50
Totally	Top 50
Toughly	Bonus (Adverbs Whose Company)
Toxic	More Words
Toxically	More Words
Tragic	More Words
Tragically	More Words
Transformationally	Bonus (Adverbs Whose Company)
Transformative	Bonus (Fancy Words)
Travesty	More Words

Tremendous	More Words
Tremendously	More Words
Tribal	Bonus (Words You Never Thought)
Tribally	Bonus (Adverbs Whose Company)
Trickily	More Words
Tricky	More Words
Trifling	More Words
Triflingly	More Words
Trite	More Words
Tritely	More Words
Trivial	More Words
Trivially	More Words
Troubled	More Words
Troublesome	More Words
Troublesomely	More Words
Troubling	More Words
Troublingly	More Words
Truly	More Words
Truncated	Bonus (Fancy Words)
Trust me/us	More Words
Truthfully	Bonus (Sentence Adverbs)
Two-bit	More Words
Two-faced	More Words
Typical	More Words
Typically	More Words

Ubiquitous	More Words
Ubiquitously	More Words
Ultimate	More Words
Ultimately	More Words, Bonus (Sentence Adverbs)
Unacceptable	More Words
Unacceptably	More Words
Unaccountable	More Words
Unaccountably	More Words
Unadorned	More Words
Unadornedly	More Words
Unadulterated	Bonus (Words To Give Your Writing)
Unarguable	More Words
Unarguably	More Words
Unashamed	More Words
Unashamedly	More Words
Unassuming	More Words
Unassumingly	More Words
Unavailing	More Words
Unavailingly	More Words
Unbearable	More Words
Unbearably	More Words
Unbelievable	More Words
Unbelievably	More Words
Unbridled	Bonus (Words You Never Thought)
Uncannily	More Words

Uncanny	More Words
Unceremonious	More Words
Unceremoniously	More Words
Uncivilly	Bonus (Adverbs Whose Company)
Unconfirmed	More Words
Unconstitutional	More Words
Unconstitutionally	More Words
Uncouthly	Bonus (Adverbs Whose Company)
Unctuous	More Words
Unctuously	More Words
Undaunted	More Words
Undauntedly	More Words
Undeniable	More Words
Undeniably	More Words
Understated	More Words
Understatedly	More Words
Undignified	More Words
Undignifiedly	More Words
Undisputed	Top 50
Undisputedly	Top 50
Undistinguishably	Bonus (Go-To Choices)
Undistinguished	More Words
Undoubted	Top 50
Undoubtedly	Top 50
Undue	More Words

Unduly	More Words
Unencumbered	More Words
Unequivocal	More Words
Unequivocally	More Words
Uneventful	More Words
Uneventfully	More Words
Unexplained	More Words
Unexplainedly	More Words
Unfair	More Words
Unfairly	More Words
Unfamiliarly	Bonus (Adverbs Whose Company)
Unfathomable	More Words
Unfathomably	More Words
Unflinching	More Words
Unflinchingly	More Words
Unfortunately	Bonus (Sentence Adverbs)
Unfoundedly	Bonus (Adverbs Whose Company)
Ungroundedly	Bonus (Adverbs Whose Company)
Unhelpful	More Words
Unhelpfully	More Words
Uniform	More Words
Uniformly	More Words
Unimaginable	More Words
Unimaginably	More Words
Uninformed	More Words

Uninformedly	More Words
Unintelligent	More Words
Unintelligently	More Words
Unintelligible	More Words
Unintelligibly	More Words
Uninterestedly	Bonus (Adverbs Whose Company)
Uninteresting	More Words
Uninterestingly	More Words
Uninterrupted	More Words
Uninterruptedly	More Words
Unique	More Words
Uniquely	More Words
Unitedly	Bonus (Adverbs Whose Company)
Universal	More Words
Universally	More Words
Unmistakable	More Words
Unmistakably	More Words
Unmitigated	More Words
Unmitigatedly	More Words
Unnecessarily	More Words
Unnecessary	More Words
Unobtrusive	More Words
Unobtrusively	More Words
Unoriginally	Bonus (Adverbs Whose Company)
Unparalleled	More Words

Unprecedented	More Words
Unprecedentedly	More Words
Unqualified	More Words
Unqualifiedly	More Words
Unquestionable	More Words
Unquestionably	More Words
Unreadably	Bonus (Adverbs Whose Company)
Unrealizably	Bonus (Adverbs Whose Company)
Unreasonable	More Words
Unreasonably	More Words
Unrelatedly	Bonus (Adverbs Whose Company)
Unreliably	Bonus (Adverbs Whose Company)
Unremarkable	More Words
Unremarkably	More Words
Unremittingly	Bonus (Adverbs Whose Company)
Unrepresentative	More Words
Unrepresentatively	More Words
Unrestrainedly	Bonus (Adverbs Whose Company)
Unrestrictedly	Bonus (Adverbs Whose Company)
Unruly	More Words
Unsatisfactorily	More Words
Unsatisfactory	More Words
Unsightly	More Words
Unsolicited	More Words
Unsophisticated	More Words

Unsophisticatedly	More Words
Unstably	Bonus (Adverbs Whose Company)
Unstoppable	More Words
Unstoppably	More Words
Unsupported	More Words
Unsure	More Words
Unsurely	More Words
Unswerving	More Words
Untenable	More Words
Untenably	More Words
Untimely	More Words
Untroubled	More Words
Unusably	Bonus (Adverbs Whose Company)
Unwieldily	More Words
Unwieldy	More Words
Unwitting	More Words
Unwittingly	More Words
Unworkable	More Words
Unworkably	More Words
Unworthily	More Words
Unworthy	More Words
Unyielding	More Words
Unyieldingly	More Words
Upon	More Words
Uppity	More Words

Upset	More Words
Upsetting	More Words
Urgent	More Words
Urgently	More Words
Useless	More Words
Uselessly	More Words
Usurped	More Words
Usurping	More Words
Utilize	More Words
Utter	More Words
Utterly	More Words
Vacuous	More Words
Vacuously	More Words
Vague	More Words
Vaguely	More Words
Valiant	More Words
Valiantly	More Words
Valid	More Words
Validly	More Words
Vast	More Words
Vast majority	More Words
Vast multitude	More Words
Vastly	More Words
Vehement	More Words
Vehemently	More Words

Venomous	Bonus (Words You Never Thought)
Verbose	More Words
Verified	Bonus (Lawyerly Words)
Verily	More Words
Verminous	Bonus (Fancy Words)
Verminy	Bonus (Fancy Words)
Very	Top 50
Very limited	More Words
Very same	More Words
Vexatious	More Words
Vexatiously	More Words
Vexed	More Words
Vexing	More Words
Vexingly	More Words
Vicarious	Bonus (Lawyerly Words)
Vicariously	Bonus (Lawyerly Words)
Vilely	Bonus (Adverbs Whose Company)
Villainous	More Words
Villainously	More Words
Violent	More Words
Violently	More Words
Virtual	More Words
Virtually	More Words
Vitiating	Bonus (Fancy Words)
Vituperative	Bonus (Fancy Words)

Vocal	More Words
Vocally	More Words
Void	Bonus (Lawyerly Words)
Voidable	Bonus (Lawyerly Words)
Volitional	Bonus (Lawyerly Words)
Volitionally	Bonus (Lawyerly Words)
Voluminous	More Words
Voluminously	More Words
Voracious	More Words
Voraciously	More Words
Vulgarly	Bonus (Adverbs Whose Company)
Wackily	More Words
Wacky	More Words
Warily	More Words
Warm	More Words
Warmly	More Words
Warranted	More Words
Warring	More Words
Wary	More Words
Wayward	More Words
Waywardly	More Words
Weak	More Words
Weakly	More Words
Wearily	More Words
Wearisome	More Words

Wearisomely	More Words
Weary	More Words
Wearying	More Words
Wearyingly	More Words
Weird	More Words
Weirdly	More Words
Well acquainted	More Words
Well aware	More Words
Well deserved	More Words
Well intentioned	More Words
Whimsical	More Words
Whimsically	More Words
Whining	More Words
Whiny	More Words
Wholesale	More Words
Wholly	Top 50
Wicked	More Words
Wickedly	More Words
Wide-eyed	More Words
Widely	More Words
Wide-ranging	More Words
Wild	More Words
Wildly	More Words
Wilful	More Words
Wilfully	More Words

Willful	More Words
Willfully	More Words
Winnowed	Bonus (Fancy Words)
Winnowing	Bonus (Fancy Words)
Wise	More Words
Wisely	More Words
Wobbly	Bonus (Words You Never Thought)
Woeful	More Words
Woefully	More Words
Wonderful	More Words
Wonderfully	More Words
Wondrously	Bonus (Adverbs Whose Company)
Worried	More Words
Worriedly	More Words
Worrisome	More Words
Worrisomely	More Words
Worrying	More Words
Worryingly	More Words
Worst-case	More Words
Worthless	More Words
Worthlessly	More Words
Worthwhile	More Words
Wretched	More Words
Wretchedly	More Words
Wrong	More Words

Wrongly	More Words
Wrought	More Words
Xenophobic	More Words
Yearning	More Words
Yearningly	More Words
Yeoman	More Words
Yet another	More Words
Yielding	More Words
Youthful	More Words
Zealous	More Words
Zealously	More Words